Feng Shui promises that once you create harmony in your home and workplace, you'll increase your peace, prosperity, happiness, health, joy, love, and luck. That's because your outer and inner worlds not only connect, but constantly influence each other.

The ancient guidelines of Feng Shui embrace all aspects of life in the most practical, detailed way. For example, Feng Shui reveals where you should live or work to attract prosperity, what sites to avoid, what shape driveway attracts money, what shape table encourages harmony, and which colors will create more peace, joy, and delight in your home.

About the Author

Selena Summers (Australia) has been writing a column on Feng Shui in the mass-market Australian magazine *Woman's Day* for ten years. Readers "Down Under" hailed *Feng Shui in 5 Minutes* as "the most easy-to-use Feng Shui book in the world."

To Write to the Author

If you wish to contact the author or would like more information about this book, please write to the author in care of Llewellyn Worldwide and we will forward your request. Both the author and publisher appreciate hearing from you and learning of your enjoyment of this book and how it has helped you. Llewellyn Worldwide cannot guarantee that every letter written to the author can be answered, but all will be forwarded. Please write to:

Selena Summers
℅ Llewellyn Worldwide
P.O. Box 64383, Dept. 0-7387-0291-9
St. Paul, MN 55164-0383, U.S.A.
Please enclose a self-addressed stamped envelope for reply,
or $1.00 to cover costs. If outside U.S.A., enclose
international postal reply coupon.

Many of Llewellyn's authors have websites with additional information and resources. For more information, please visit our website at:

http://www.llewellyn.com

FENG SHUI
in
5 MINUTES

SELENA SUMMERS

Llewellyn Publications
St. Paul, Minnesota

FIRST EDITION
Second Printing, 2004

Book design and editing by Michael Maupin
Cover art © 2002 by PhotoDisc
Cover design by Lisa Novak
Illustration on p. 26 courtesy of Adele Summers
Interior illustrations by Kevin R. Brown

Library of Congress Cataloging-in-Publication Data

Summers, Selena, 1945–
    Feng shui in 5 minutes / Selena Summers. —1st ed.
        p.   cm.
    Includes index.
    ISBN 0-7387-0291-9
    1. Feng shui. I. Title: Feng shui in five minutes. II. Title.

BF1779.F4 S845 2002
133.3'337—dc21   2002030061

Llewellyn Worldwide does not participate in, endorse, or have any authority or responsibility concerning private business transactions between our authors and the public.
    All mail addressed to the author is forwarded but the publisher cannot, unless specifically instructed by the author, give out an address or phone number.
    Any Internet references contained in this work are current at publication time, but the publisher cannot guarantee that a specific location will continue to be maintained. Please refer to the publisher's website for links to authors' websites and other sources.

Llewellyn Publications
A Division of Llewellyn Worldwide, Ltd.
P.O. Box 64383, Dept. 0-7387-0291-9
St. Paul, MN 55164-0383, U.S.A.
www.llewellyn.com

♻ Printed in the United States of America on recycled paper

This is for Jack and Adele Summers, my parents,
who always gave books a place of honor
in our home.

Contents

Chapter One

Welcome to the Mysterious Art of Feng Shui

the basics

What is this mysterious art of Feng Shui?

Have you ever wondered why you felt happier or more at home in one place than another? What you felt is good Feng Shui. And have you ever felt strangely uneasy in another place, but couldn't explain why? What you felt is bad Feng Shui (also known as *sha qi*).

Nearly everyone is surprised to discover they have in fact experienced good or bad Feng Shui. Indeed, most people know of a house that seems to shower all who live there with either good or bad luck.

Yet, Feng Shui is more than just good or bad atmosphere.

It concerns the energy of a place. You'll hear a hundred different definitions. Some call it the Chinese art of arranging furniture and homes to encourage wealth and health. Others call it earthly astrology.

One famous definition is the "Ancient Chinese Art of Placement." That's because Feng Shui seeks the most harmonious place for everything in the universe from your bed, desk, or kitchen stove, to your house on a hillside. Feng Shui philosophy covers a vast area.

The simplest definition? Feng Shui aims to increase harmony in your environment.

How can Feng Shui improve my life?

Feng Shui promises that once you create harmony in your home, workplace, and surroundings you'll increase your peace, prosperity, happiness, health, joy, love, and luck. That's because your outer and inner worlds not only connect, but constantly influence each other.

The ancient guidelines of Feng Shui embrace all aspects of life in the most practical, detailed way. For example, Feng Shui reveals where you should live or work to attract prosperity, what sites to avoid, which driveway shape attracts money, what shape table encourages harmony, and which colors will create more peace, joy, and delight in your home.

Even modern psychology agrees with many aspects of Feng Shui. Some architects ask if the puzzling "sick building syndrome," in which certain occupants suffer baffling tiredness and upsets, is just another name for bad Feng Shui.

Ahem—I want to get richer. Can Feng Shui help?

Yes! The ancient Chinese wise men were as interested as we are in getting richer. Feng Shui tells you about secret "money magnet" sites that invite wealth to come to you, or where to find the Golden Prosperity Point in your house, what driveway shapes attract riches, or how a view of bare walls repels wealth, and what house designs send money running out the backdoor faster than it can come in.

You'll discover hundreds of little-known tips to rush prosperity to your doorstep.

What do the words Feng Shui mean?

Feng means "wind," and *Shui* means "water." Some say this is because Feng Shui is as unfathomable as wind and water. Others say it's because wind (qi life energy, or spirit) and water provide the basis of all new creation. They are the hidden elemental powers that influence human destiny.

How is Feng Shui pronounced?

I pronounce it "Fung *Shway*" as this sounds to me like the Mandarin pronunciation. Cantonese and other pronunciations sound like "Foong Shwee,"

"Foong Shoy," "Fong Soy," or even "Fooong Swee." Don't worry too much because there are at least eight major dialects in China, and many sound as different from standard Chinese or Mandarin as French and German do from English!

When and where did Feng Shui begin?

Feng Shui originated way back in the mists of time. Scholars differ on dates, but recent archaeological excavations suggest between the second and fourth century B.C. in China as a likely beginning. In fact, the first compass was invented in China not for navigation, but for the purposes of Feng Shui.

In the early days of the art, Feng Shui Grandmasters exclusively advised the Chinese emperors and were carried to sites in sedan chairs. They guarded their knowledge jealously, and much of Feng Shui sought to find an auspicious or fortunate burial place for the privileged few.

As time passed, interest switched to finding places to bring luck, happiness, and good fortune to the living. Many ancient sites like the Forbidden City in Peking (now called Beijing) were laid out according to Feng Shui principles, and one of the first books on Feng Shui appeared, *The Yellow Emperor's Dwelling Classic.*

In imperial times it was possible for people to sue each other for infringing the rules of good Feng Shui. During British rule in Hong Kong, millions of dollars were paid in compensation to people who claimed their good Feng Shui was damaged by government buildings or roads.

Where do people practice Feng Shui today?

As Chinese culture traveled, so did Feng Shui—at first through the East. Recently, the Feng Shui craze has spread like wildfire around the Western world.

Film stars and celebrities now track down Feng Shui experts to help harmonize their lives and mansions. Everyone from Catherine Zeta-Jones to *X-Files* TV star David Duchovny to British billionaire Richard Branson applies its powerful remedies.

In London, top soccer teams follow Feng Shui principles. In Australia, casinos design their buildings with Feng Shui in mind, and international businesses apply Feng Shui guidelines to boost their profits. From Paris to New York, people flock to learn the secrets of this fascinating art.

Of course, the home of Feng Shui is still Hong Kong, where even before a building is constructed a Feng Shui expert joins the design team. In Hong Kong, if you see a house left empty for no apparent reason it's probably a case of bad Feng Shui. No one will live there, no matter how high the demand for housing.

Singapore has a strong tradition of Feng Shui, while some Eastern countries like Japan and Thailand practice a slightly different form.

Does the ancient art of Feng Shui suit our modern world?

You bet! Wouldn't you like to possess more energy and vitality? Wouldn't you like to increase your harmony, health, wealth, happiness, joy, and luck?

Also, as modern life becomes increasingly stressful, more people want to create a haven of comfort in their homes. We all want our homes to be happy places where we can recharge our batteries.

The ancient wisdom of the Chinese has been stored by sages over thousands of years. Why not keep an open mind and benefit from their carefully collected secrets?

Does Feng Shui connect with intuition?

Yes. For instance, the famous Feng Shui warning to always note the first impression you get when you walk into a building or place links closely to intuition. One entire branch of Feng Shui is even called the "Intuitive school."

Most women pick up Feng Shui very easily because they often use their natural intuition. But anyone who studies Feng Shui will become more intuitive. Start by noting which living and workspaces energize you, and which ones drain or upset you.

How many different Feng Shui schools exist?

Quite a few. Feng Shui embraces such a huge area, it's only natural that as centuries passed different schools or branches sprang up. Each emphasizes a slightly different area.

For instance, the "Form school" deals more with shapes, the "Compass school" concentrates on compass directions, and the "Nine Stars school" makes great use of ancient Nine Star astrology. The more modern Intuitive school is self-explanatory.

Dragon Door Feng Shui is an international type of Feng Shui. Based on ancient, classic texts, it makes use of intuition, too. Dragon Door Feng Shui offers one huge advantage—it applies in both Northern and Southern Hemispheres as its principles focus on the existing position of doors.

Many Feng Shui books confuse me, especially their complex tables and rules on compass directions. What is the easiest, most practical method?

You're holding it in your hands! Dragon Door Feng Shui.

People write to my Feng Shui column in *Woman's Day* magazine, Australia, from all over the world to say how difficult they find some Feng Shui books.

If you are a fabulously wealthy emperor or tycoon, you can no doubt arrange to live in a home with the front door facing a certain compass direction. But most people need to be practical.

That's why this book uses the easy-to-follow but powerful Dragon Door Feng Shui principles, outlined by Professor Vincent Wu, a former Grandmaster of Hong Kong with whom I studied for many years.

One of the world's leading Feng Shui consultants, Professor Wu is celebrated for the brilliant way he adapted age-old Eastern principles to suit modern Western ways. Although Professor Wu consulted with international banks, multinational companies, and barons of industry, his Feng Shui methods adapt equally well to domestic homes, gardens, offices, and workplaces anywhere in the world.

What are Yin and Yang?

Yin and Yang are the two basic opposite forces in the universe which together form a balanced whole. They constantly interact to create all things and appeared when the invisible life force first divided in two.

Yin is often represented as female, night, moon, passive, dark, cold, and softness. Yang is often represented as male, day, active, light, heat, and hard-ness. Yet each force carries the seed of the opposite force within.

What is qi or chi?

You'll find the term *qi* or *chi* (pronounced "chee") right throughout all Feng Shui. In Japan, it's called *ki*.

Qi is best translated as life energy, vitality, cosmic breath, or the invisible life force. This concept appears in all branches of Chinese art and philosophy, poetry, acupuncture, martial arts, herbal medicine, and the famous physical exercises Qi-gong. Qi divides into the Five Elements.

What are the Five Elements?

Qi life energy can be classified into five basic patterns, moods, qualities, or types called Metal, Water, Wood, Fire, and Earth. These qualities make up all matter, but the names are symbolic rather than representing the common substances we all know. The Five Elements always control or nourish each other in a fixed order.

Feng Shui originated in the Northern Hemisphere, but I live in the Southern Hemisphere. Do I need different guidelines?

With many schools of Feng Shui you would, and certain principles would reverse. However, as mentioned before, this book outlines Dragon Door Feng Shui, which applies internationally. It does not depend on compass directions at all.

Does a person's birth year change his or her Feng Shui?

Knowing your birthdate often enables an expert to fine-tune your Feng Shui to the last degree. But first things first. Right now it's more important that this book gives you a solid understanding of the vital, basic principles of Feng Shui.

Is Feng Shui connected to "Earth magic" or geomancy?

Often the two terms are used interchangeably, but I feel Feng Shui covers a much wider field than geomancy. Some experts restrict the term geomancy to fortunetelling by means of a figure made when randomly throwing a handful of earth.

Chapter Two

The Nine
Celestial Cures

an easy guide

What are the Nine Celestial Cures?

The Nine Celestial Cures are nine ways of adjusting qi life energy for your benefit as it moves through your house, garden, workplace, or even your body. Feng Shui explains that problems arise when qi life energy moves too fast, or slows to a trickle or blocks entirely. Happily, the Celestial Cures enable you to alter the flow, and transform your working and living space.

How can this "qi key" unlock the benefits for me to enjoy?

Once you understand how the Nine Celestial Cures affect energy movement, you can create a more harmonious home life and pep up your prosperity, health, and personal sparkle. You'll have fun experimenting with do-it-yourself Feng Shui.

At first some ideas may seem strange. But you'll soon find you can apply them using your intuition and common sense.

How do the Nine Celestial Cures improve the flow of qi life energy in my house, workplace, or garden?

Each of the nine classes of cures affects qi life energy differently. Some cures, like wind chimes, stir up, then harmonize energy. Other cures, like heavy statues placed on either side of an overly large doorway, block, or slow the movement of energy. Yet another class of cures, like mirrors, reflects energy into a different direction.

Lights add to existing energy while other Cures transform energy to higher levels. Crystals protect and purify existing energy as they absorb sha qi, or bad energy. Some of the strongest Celestial Cures perform more than one function.

What is the First Celestial Cure?

Mirrors top this category of cures, which encompasses all kinds of reflectors and lights. Lamps, chandeliers, shiny ribbons, and most reflective surfaces are included. Sparkling clear quartz crystals (often called solidified light) play a huge part, too.

How can a mirror provide an exit for blocked energy?

If you live in a small apartment, motor home, or boat with a front door but no back door, hang a mirror in order to create an artificial back door or energy exit. You will feel the transformed atmosphere at once. Prove this by removing the mirror. Right away the area will feel "closed-in" again.

Mirrors are used so much they are called the "aspirin" of the Feng Shui medicine bag. Choose large wall mirrors rather than mirror tiles because tiles fragment images. A "whole" image is always more harmonious.

How does adding a light to a room or house increase harmonious energy?

Here's an example. Everyone knows a dark entrance to a house tends to make visitors feel gloomy. The place seems uninviting. Feng Shui goes further and says adding another light actually increases harmonious qi life energy.

That's why a common Celestial Cure for a problem L-shaped house is to add a garden light to "square off" or rebalance the irregular shape, or missing section.

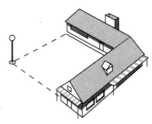

Why is a chandelier a powerful Feng Shui remedy?

Chandeliers combine crystals and light. Also, their shape usually follows graceful flowing curves, rather than straight lines. This makes them a very strong Feng Shui Cure. So it's not surprising that today a growing number of natural healers feature chandeliers in reception and treatment rooms.

What is the Second Celestial Cure?

Goldfish are the Second Celestial Cure. Worldwide, Feng Shui experts use this most powerful cure to add harmonious energy to a room or workplace. That's the reason you'll often see a tank of goldfish in Chinese restaurants. Dentists who place goldfish in waiting rooms to calm nervous patients are intuitively creating good Feng Shui.

Where should I place goldfish in my home?

Goldfish can be placed almost anywhere to increase peace, harmony, and wealth. Use your intuition to decide where. But goldfish are particularly helpful to neutralize bad energy directed at your house by a neighbor's pointy roof eave.

A lonely female executive, recently transferred from Melbourne to Sydney for a great new job, wrote to me that she hated to come home in the evenings to her lifeless, empty apartment. She felt depressed and was thinking of resigning. But after she bought a bowl containing two darting goldfish (she called them Feng and Shui) her apartment gained a lovely new feeling of life. As she fed her fish while watching their soothing movements, she felt happier and more at home.

Recently, she wrote to say she had made a delightful male friend in an apartment in the same building. They met in the elevator when he offered to carry the large sack of fish food she was struggling to carry!

Which fish bowl shapes are luckiest?

Any fish tank brings good fortune, and is better than no fish. But a round, curved or octagonal bowl invites much better Feng Shui than a square or rectangular bowl.

You'll find many pet shops carry octagonal bowls now that Feng Shui is so popular. Be sure there's enough room for your fish—don't cram a huge number into a tiny space. Three or six fish is a happy number for a small apartment. Larger homes can be more adventurous.

What does the death of a goldfish mean?

When a goldfish dies for no logical reason such as neglect, lack of food, or poor quality water, the dead fish has absorbed bad luck coming your way. In the East some people include one black fish specifically for this reason. As soon as possible, check your bowl environment setup with a pet shop, then replace your dead fish.

What is the Third Celestial Cure?

Would you believe that scraggy old Spot and Fluffy, your lovable family dog or cat, is actually a Celestial Cure? It's true. _Pets_ of any kind, whether furred or feathered, instantly increase harmonious energy in a home or workplace.

Does this mean a home with a pet is luckier and more harmonious than one without?

Yes! So if your home lacks luck, point yourself in the direction of a pet shop. It's no surprise that modern psychology agrees pets improve and calm the atmosphere in homes, hospitals, nursing homes, and prisons. According to researchers from New York State University, owning a pet even lowers your blood pressure. Door-to-door salesmen also report that homes with pets have a happier atmosphere than those without.

What is the Fourth Celestial Cure?

Harmonious sounds make up the Fourth Celestial Cure. These include tinkling bells, wind chimes, birdsong, running water, wind whispering through bamboo or trees, the sounds of gentle raindrops falling on the roof, humming insects, and melodious music.

Is one style of wind chime luckier than others?

Some Feng Shui experts prefer a wind chime with hollow rods, as these encourage qi life energy to flow upward. However, modern intuitive Feng Shui says simply select a wind chime that you find attractive. This means the wind chime is attuned to your personal energy field.

Why are wind chimes such a powerful universal cure?

Simple as they seem, wind chimes combine several powerful cures—harmonious sounds, gentle motion and the wind, or "Feng," which is so basic to Feng Shui. Wind is also a prime form of qi life energy, sometimes called cosmic breath or spirit.

So when you hang a wind chime in your home, you introduce harmony, spirit, and motion. These are three mighty cosmic forces, with the power to transform unpleasant conditions.

If birdsong increases good Feng Shui, how do I attract more birds to my garden?

Place a birdbath, birdfeeder, or dish of clean water somewhere up high, away from prowling cats. After a while, birds will flock and some may become quite tame.

Many people in Australia love to handfeed pigeons or warbling magpies in their garden. It's fun to watch magpies, who become so tame they knock on your window for daily scraps. Later you can enjoy watching these birds bring new young members of their family to join in this ritual.

Bees hum in my garden. Is this a sign of good fortune?

The humming of insects, including bees, is a sound with particularly good Feng Shui. But the sound of people screeching from bee stings is bad Feng Shui. So be careful!

What is the Fifth Celestial Cure?

Color is the Fifth Celestial Cure, and provides a quick way to transform a room with bad energy. Beware of all-white exteriors and interiors. They drain energy and signify mourning unless you add splashes of bright color like cherry or red. Cream invites much better Feng Shui than white.

I need a quick, easy hint on choosing a room or house color with good Feng Shui.

For house interiors, pale pastels radiate the best Feng Shui and surround you with harmonious energy. If you live in a cool climate, pale peach, apricot, terra cotta, lemon, yellow, or pink hues prove cheering. In a warm climate, you may prefer cooler pastels like blue, turquoise, lavender, or pale green. Go with your intuition—it's very close to Feng Shui.

If you're really stuck, use a pendulum to decide between two colors. Chapter 14 tells you how to make and use the pendulum.

What is the Sixth Celestial Cure?

Plants and flowers make up the Sixth Celestial Cure, bringing enlivening energy to a room. Placed under a staircase, a green plant helps healthy qi life energy rise to the next floor.

If the energy around your office desk feels stale and lifeless (especially if the room is crammed with computers and fluorescent lights), add a green plant. You'll instantly feel better. If you remove the plant for watering, the will area feel dead again.

Are some plants less auspicious or lucky than others?

Yes. When setting up a Prosperity Plant in your house or workplace (the next chapter tells how), a round-leaf plant like a maranta or jade makes an excellent choice. A pointy-leaf plant like an azalea tends to repel luck.

In an office, a spider plant (*Chlorophytum comosum*) absorbs "electronic smog" near computers and office machinery. This nifty little plant reproduces itself almost as fast as a photocopier copies! Recent research by the U.S. National Aeronautics and Space Administration (NASA) confirms that certain live green plants remove toxins and pollutants from interiors. It's fascinating how often modern science confirms age-old Feng Shui principles.

Why should I avoid dried flowers or plants in my house?

Dried flowers and plants bring the aura of death into a home. Traditionally they are not considered good Feng Shui. If you love dried flowers, your good feeling toward the flowers does lessen the bad effect a little.

But keep dried flowers away from your front door and room entrances. Where possible, display them in a hobby room toward the back of your house, and hang a sparkling clear crystal quartz nearby, as a balance. One cure is to keep dried flowers in a crystal vase, as crystal is good Feng Shui, and helps neutralize problem energy.

Why do silk flowers and plants invite good Feng Shui?

Silk flowers and plants are good Feng Shui because silk is a revered natural fiber and everlasting silk flowers and plants connect with the idea of eternal life.

Plastic flowers are bad Feng Shui because they are not made from a natural fabric. I'm sure your intuition tells you this.

What is the Seventh Celestial Cure?

Moving Items make up the seventh group of Celestial Cures. Items such as fountains, wind vanes, mobiles, windmills, whirligigs, grandfather clocks, flag bunting, and moving lights all appear in this list. You can see that as fountains, wind chimes, and moving lights qualify for several categories of Celestial Cures, they must indeed be powerful remedies.

Cures that move in a harmonious circular direction invite still better Feng Shui. That's why you'll find rotary doors and rotary overhead fans included as Celestial Cures.

Why is a grandfather clock good Feng Shui?

Many people intuitively feel grandfather clocks add stability, character, and warmth to a home—just like grandpa used to! If you're feeling insecure from too many moves, add one to your home and see how much better you feel. They're also a favorite item to hand down as a cherished family heirloom.

Feng Shui experts explain that the gentle movement of the pendulum adds qi life energy to your house.

Position your grandfather clock so it's not visible from the front door. It's usually best on the "Dragon side," or left-hand side of your house, when you stand at your front door looking out. But if you have a strong urge to place it elsewhere, follow your intuition.

How can I attract more customers to my shop using the Seventh Celestial Cure?

If the entrance to your shop feels lifeless, customers will feel no inclination to enter. You'll attract more business if you stir up the qi life energy around your door with a Celestial Cure that features movement.

Use your common sense. A florist or plant shop may benefit from a display of wind chimes or whirligigs painted like flowers near the door. But an ice cream shop might attract more customers with moving lights.

In a dress shop, you might increase customer interest in a winter display with a fan that blows fake snow around mannequins. In the window of a financial organization, a fan whirling imitation currency will stir up qi life energy and attract customers.

What is the Eighth Celestial Cure?

Heavy Objects make up the Eighth Celestial Cure. They consist of items like large wooden screens, statues, stones, or sculptures. These either block or deflect unwanted or overly fast energy.

Statues can also be used to rebalance uneven shapes like an L-shaped house, in the same way a garden light is used.

How might I use statues to stabilize qi life energy running too quickly into my house through our double front door?

If your front door is too large for the size of your home or workplace, occupants will receive too much qi life energy. They'll quarrel and become jumpy.

Two large statues placed either side of the door (perhaps lions, dogs, or any theme that appeals) will cut off some of the excess energy rushing through the entrance. Residents will then become calmer and less prone to misfortune.

What is the Ninth Celestial Cure?

Musical Instruments make up the Ninth Celestial Cure, and of these flutes stand out as the most important. Bamboo flutes are among the oldest musical instrument known to humankind, but flutes made from bird bone or reeds date way back as well.

Placed anywhere in your home, flutes give spiritual protection. Today, you can select flutes made from crystal, glass, wood, silver, precious metals, and many other materials.

Strangely enough, hand fans appear in this ninth category, too. Some old documents say the mere presence of these romantic items invites unheard music. Other manuscripts refer to fans as wind instruments, due to the soft *"ssshhh"* of a fan being opened, or gently waved. Their semicircular shape is also lucky.

Why does a fan encourage romance, when placed at the correct position in a room?

Many cultures—from Chinese to Japanese, Spanish, and Portuguese—instinctively link the fan with romance, flirting, and elegant females.

That's why the fan—which has intrinsic good Feng Shui—encourages romance when placed at the correct position, the I Ching Ba-Gua Marriage Point in your living room. (The next chapter will explain these positions in detail.)

I bought a wall light shaped like a fan. Can I combine Celestial Cures for more power?

Yes. A fan wall light adds harmonious energy to a place in the form of light. The fan shape gives extra good Feng Shui and luck.

Why are flutes the most powerful musical instrument?

Flutes carry more power than all other musical instruments because of their spiritual significance and hollow shape, which channels qi life energy upward.

How should flutes be positioned for extra good luck?

Two flutes are even more powerful than one. To position them in a house for protection and good Feng Shui, place them anywhere you feel sha qi or bad energy, such as on exposed beams. Otherwise, near a front entrance is a good position.

Always place flutes with mouthpieces pointing downward, preferably slanted like an inverted V. Tie them with red ribbons or red tassels for extra good fortune.

Psssst! I've heard whispers of a Tenth Earthly Cure. Are they true?

Yes. Modern Feng Shui masters continually adapt ancient principles to fix problems of today. That's why many Feng Shui Masters now use the electronic energy of items from television sets and radios to computers. There's no doubt they provide energy, too.

I'm amazed to hear that radio, television, or computers can be a Feng Shui cure. How can I prove this?

Do you have a room no one uses? No doubt it feels lifeless. Now add a radio, computer, or television and leave it on for a while each day. You'll discover the atmosphere in the room completely changes. It will feel more alive due to the energy from the Tenth Earthly Cure.

Knowledge is power. You'll find that knowing about the Tenth Cure can be unexpectedly useful at times.

Please sum up the Nine Celestial Cures in an easy chart.

First: *Reflectors and Lights*—mirrors, chandeliers, shiny ribbons, crystals

Second: *Goldfish*

Third: *Household Pets*

Fourth: *Harmonious Sounds*—tinkling bells, wind chimes, birdsong, humming insects, whispering wind in bamboo, raindrops and running water

Fifth: *Color*

Sixth: *Plants and Flowers*—natural and silk

Seventh: *Moving Items*—fountains, wind vanes, windmills, rotary doors, rotary fans, grandfather clocks, flag bunting, mobiles, whirligigs, moving lights

Eighth: *Heavy Objects*—statues, stones

Ninth: *Musical Instruments*—flute, fans

Wind whispering through bamboo
by Adele Summers

**Harmonious Sounds—
one of the Nine Celestial Cures**

Chapter Three

Ancient Secrets of the Ba-Gua

*activating the sectors for
romance, prosperity & more*

**What is the Ba-Gua? Where did
it originate?**

The Ba-Gua is an ancient technique you can use to transform and enrich your life. The word literally means "eight sides" and is pronounced "Baa-Gwah."

In practice, the Ba-Gua is an eight-sided symbol of eight life treasures: Prosperity, Fame, Marriage and Relationships, Children, Helpful People, Career, Wisdom, and Family/Health.

How does the Ba-Gua connect to the famous I Ching or "Chinese Book of Changes"?

The Ba-Gua is a visual interpretation or octagonal symbol of the ancient I Ching book, with its philosophy of interconnectedness and its eight trigrams (see illustration below).

Many readers will have consulted the I Ching, the oldest book of guidance in the world, by asking a question and then throwing coins. The resulting coin pattern then refers you to an answer in the book, which usually stuns you with its wisdom. No wonder the I Ching is often called the "mother of Chinese thought."

How can I use the Ba-Gua to enhance my life?

Feng Shui consultants often superimpose this octagonal symbol on rooms, houses, or blocks of land to

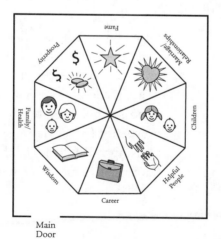

Main
Door

obtain a reading on your current life and luck, plus your future destiny. They "balance" or "strengthen" problem areas with Celestial Cures or lucky objects placed in the correct position.

After this, expect to see an improvement in your life within one cycle of the moon—roughly one month.

I'm new to Eastern ideas, and the Ba-Gua seems rather strange. How can it possibly work?

The Ba-Gua works because all creation is one swirling mass of qi life energy, and your inner world and outer world are connected—a thought increasingly accepted by modern psychology. What you think and your whole state of being reflects in the physical world closest to you—your home. Nothing is separate or disconnected. Even the famous French designer Coco Chanel said "an interior is the natural projection of the soul."

It follows that if you make a positive energy change to your immediate physical surroundings, you then positively affect other areas of your life.

How do I choose lucky objects to activate each of the eight Ba-Gua areas or treasures?

With some areas of the Ba-Gua, such as Prosperity, lucky items are laid down quite strictly. But with most areas, you can pick any small item in the cosmically correct colors that feels right to you. This means the item will be in harmony with your individual energy field, your home, and your needs.

For instance, imagine you want more Helpful People dropping by as friends to assist you on special matters. It might be appropriate to buy two special coffee mugs in the cosmically correct colors of black and white, then keep them at the correct place on a Ba-Gua.

Another person might see a tiny white sculpture of two friends shaking hands and feel this symbolizes Helpful People. The statuette could be placed on a black plate, or a black shiny ribbon positioned alongside. Use your intuition and imagination.

What special colors activate each area of the Ba-Gua?

Here's a handy chart:

Ba-Gua Area	*Activating Cosmic Colors*
Prosperity:	Red and green
Fame:	Yellow, red, and green
Marriage/Relationships:	Red and white
Children:	Black, white, and yellow or lemon
Helpful People:	Black and white
Career:	Black, green, and white
Wisdom:	Green and black
Family/Health:	Black, red, and green

I'd love to hear some success stories from your Ba-Gua reader file . . . starting with prosperity.

After setting up a Ba-Gua, many, many people have written thank-you letters to tell of sudden promotions, gifts, unexpected inheritances, bonuses, financial windfalls, and lottery and raffle wins. Not to mention new babies, marriages, new romances, and other happy events. Naturally, due to privacy, only very general indications can be given of their situations.

One amusing letter that sticks in my mind concerns a woman who suddenly seemed so lucky all her friends demanded cuttings from her Prosperity Plant! Another gentleman who strengthened both Wisdom and Prosperity won a car, money, and other prizes on a well-known TV quiz show. And many people have won overseas holidays and other delights in competitions. "I entered heaps of competitions, but until I set up a Ba-Gua, I won nothing," wrote a teenager from New Zealand. She sent a photo of herself and her family in the brand-new speedboat she had won.

. . . Or protection?

One enterprising Aussie woman with her own business wrote how she placed a flute over her legal papers, which she kept in the Wisdom area. She was worried that an impending court case might bankrupt her. What a thrilling surprise when, out of the blue, she received notification that legal action was withdrawn and the case was dropped!

. . . Or Helpful People?

Another favorite letter concerns an artist with a studio alongside a block of apartments whose rental tenants proved extremely noisy, making it difficult for him to paint. When one lot of tenants moved out, the next lot seemed just as noisy, or even worse. Finally the artist's wife set up a Ba-Gua with black and white ribbons to activate Helpful People.

About two weeks later, a large "For Sale" billboard went up outside the apartments. "It was printed in black and white instead of the usual color job. I wondered if there was a connection," mused the artist's wife.

The apartment block was auctioned then resold as own-your-own apartments. This time the neighbors were different—house-proud and quiet. The artist jumped for joy, though he half-suspected a coincidence. (Feng Shui says coincidences don't exist.)

. . . Or romance?

Another lonely young woman, whom I will call Christine, wrote that she had placed a fan at her Ba-Gua Marriage area and waited hopefully for some good luck. None arrived. Instead, three weeks later her roommate's new puppy crawled up on the couch, and chewed and swallowed the red tassel hanging from the fan. In a panic, both girls rushed the pup to an all-night emergency vet. The handsome young vet turned out to be rather taken with Christine. Now they're engaged. And I'm not surprised that she plans to carry a small lace fan along with her wedding bouquet on the big day.

The Chinese—the oldest, wisest, continuous civilization in the world—have practiced Feng Shui for thousands and thousands of years. Why do they keep applying it today if it doesn't work?

Does the Ba-Gua symbol work best in certain rooms?

For a general life reading, apply the Ba-Gua in your living room or, as a second choice, your bedroom. A reading in your office or workplace usually gives fascinating insights, too. For homes on blocks of land, a Ba-Gua reading on the entire site often proves revealing.

We have both a lounge and family room rather than a single living room. Which one is best for applying a Ba-Gua?

Choose the room that feels most like the "heart" of your house. Don't select the kitchen, even if you spend most of your time there. That's because Feng Shui views your house as a living body, and each part corresponds with a section of this body. (The kitchen is viewed as the stomach of your home.)

If a room has several doors, how do you tell which is the main entrance?

Consider which door is used most often, or which door is larger. A door added later is often seen as a secondary door. Use your intuition—it's your home and you should be able to figure it out. If it helps, ask everyone in your home for an opinion.

What are the steps to set up a Ba-Gua in a room?
Does it matter which direction my room faces?

Forget about the direction your room faces—with international Dragon Door Feng Shui, as taught in this book, all positions start from the existing main door to a room. Don't worry about compass directions.

First, leave eight grains of rice in a small container overnight on the floor by the main door to your room. This informs the universe you're setting up a Ba-Gua. (Some Feng Shui experts leave out this step, but I find you enjoy better results if you include it.)

Next, figure out where the eight Life Situations of the Ba-Gua will be in your individual room. The illustration below will help. Always start by imagining the bottom section of the octagonal symbol—containing Wisdom, Career, or Helpful People—on the wall containing the main door to your room.

If your door is in the middle of your wall, it will sit in the Career Position of your Ba-Gua. If your door is to the left, it will sit in the Wisdom section and if your door is to the right it will lie in the Helpful People position.

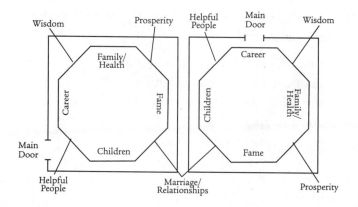

Remember, once you line up this bottom section, the other Life Situations of the Ba-Gua always follow in the same order.

I've lined up the Ba-Gua in my house. What next?

Once you've lined up the fateful eight Ba-Gua areas in your room, you can "balance the Ba-Gua" to improve your luck and lot in life.

For example, if you hope to marry or improve your relationship, the previous list shows that the Marriage area colors are red and white. You might then place red flowers in a white vase at the Ba-Gua Marriage area, to strengthen this section of your life. Or you might feel happier placing a photo of you and your beloved in a red and white frame at this Ba-Gua position.

Pssst! I need money fast. How do I find the Prosperity area?

The Ba-Gua Prosperity section in a room is always the top left-hand corner diagonally opposite the main door to your room. Check the two illustrations and you'll soon catch on.

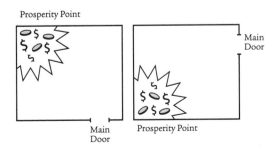

Many people call this the Golden Prosperity Point, but it's more an area than one point.

What colors and lucky objects activate the Prosperity area?

As the previous list shows, red and green are the special colors for the Ba-Gua Prosperity area. It's traditional to place a green plant here with rounded leaves, like a maranta. Forget sharp or pointy-leaf plants, like azaleas.

Next, wrap a few coins in red paper and place them under the plant. Now, expect the best because, as your plant grows so will your money! Take care of your plant, and replace it if it withers. Does your Prosperity area receive very little light? Rotate two Prosperity Plants—one outside, one inside. A good quality artificial plant is fine, too, such as a silk plant. But avoid tacky-looking plastic plants.

I'm an actor. Can I use the Ba-Gua to attract fame, or at least become better known?

I receive numerous letters from actors wanting to use the Ba-Gua to help achieve fame.

Placing a red, yellow, and green lamp at the Fame spot is especially helpful. But one aspiring television actress I know preferred a photo of herself in a red and green frame near a yellow lamp. Later she was offered a juicy income as a regular in a popular Australian television serial.

If you have a small business, you may prefer to become well-known for your excellent products. A video mail-order businessman keeps one of his videos wrapped in the three correct colors, in the Fame area of the Ba-Gua in his office. "Business is booming!" he says.

How do I use the Ba-Gua to encourage romance, marriage, or good relationships?

To encourage a new romance, you might place a red fan tied with a white ribbon at the Marriage/Relationships area.

One married woman, who wanted to harmonize her rocky marriage, decided to move her piano out of the spare room (a dangerous place, as you'll discover later) to the Marriage/Relationship area of her lounge. She also kept a white vase of red flowers on the piano. She said as her relationship was in huge trouble, a huge Feng Shui cure like a piano seemed a good idea.

Shortly after she moved the piano, her relationship with her husband began to improve. "We used to watch television night after night, and never talk. Now he often asks me to play the piano instead. He even hums along! Recently we moved the television into the spare room and turned it into a sunroom. We're planning a second honeymoon now. . ."

I'd love more helpful people to appear in my life. How can I activate this area of the Ba-Gua?

First, leave eight grains of rice in your lounge doorway overnight.

Check back to the color table, and you'll notice black and white are the special colors for this area.

So place any black and white item that feels suitable in the right-hand corner of the wall containing the main door to your room.

For example, one young girl complained she was new in town and needed helpful new people as contacts. She moved her white telephone to the Helpful People spot and placed a new black phone number book alongside, with a striped black and white pen. Soon her phone rang so often she moved it elsewhere to get some peace!

My child's career seems troubled. How do I use the Ba-Gua to attract harmony or promotion?

Place your child's photo in a black and green frame at the Wisdom area of the Ba-Gua. Or perhaps you might choose another small, activating item related to your child's work.

Help! Our family fights so often we almost need a referee. How do I apply the Ba-Gua to create a more harmonious family situation?

Place eight grains of rice in the lounge doorway overnight. You might decide the situation is so bad you'd better position a really powerful Celestial Cure at the Family/Health position.

Tie a flute with red, green, and black ribbons. Then place it halfway along the wall to the left of the wall containing your main room door. This is the Family/Health position.

My health worries me. How do I activate the Ba-Gua to encourage favorable cosmic forces?

> If you feel stressed or worried about your health, keep a round or octagonal bowl of goldfish at the Ba-Gua Family/Health position. Perhaps choose six red fish and one black fish. Then you might place a small green treasure chest in the bottom of the fish tank to complete the Family/Health colors of red, green, and black. Spend a little time each day sitting near this position watching the soothing movements of your lucky fish.

My L-shaped living room means one area of the Ba-Gua is missing. *Ooops*—**it's Marriage! No wonder I'm single! Is there a cure?**

> Now you can see why the Chinese dislike odd-shaped and especially L-shaped rooms. They usually mean one section of the Ba-Gua will be missing, giving residents problems in this life situation.
>
> The illustration shows remedies applicable to most L-shaped rooms.
>
> Note how hanging a mirror on one edge of your missing room section expands the room's energy out into the missing section. There's a certain logic here, and this general principle is often used in Feng Shui.

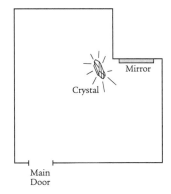

Mirror

Crystal

Main Door

If possible, choose a round, oval or octagonal mirror. But a square or rectangular mirror is better than none. Another cure is to hang a crystal where illustrated to correct the energy flow.

Check how the room feels now. You may decide to further strengthen the Marriage area of your Ba-Gua by adding another Celestial Cure nearby, such as a fan or a plant, in the correct I Ching Marriage colors of red and white. Your plant, for instance, might feature red flowers in a white ornamental pot.

Horrors! My L-shaped living room means I have no Prosperity area. Is this the cause of my money worries?

Very likely, but relax as Feng Shui offers several remedies. You could follow the previous basic rule of hanging a mirror to extend the room's energy into the "missing section."

Then place your green prosperity plant near the mirror, with the three coins underneath the plant wrapped in red paper. The bigger your plant grows the better for your money.

A second idea? Add another Celestial Cure that appeals, such as a red and green lamp. See the chapter on cures (page 11) and decide for yourself.

Do a fireplace and chimney at my Prosperity area cause a money leak? Tell me the cure—*and hurry!*

An open fireplace with chimney at the Prosperity area sends money energy whirling up the chimney. Place a mirror above the mantelpiece, or near this area, to prevent money loss. A hardy green plant is a second choice. (Wherever positioned, a chimney will cause an energy leak at that particular Life Situation.)

Does a second door at a certain Ba-Gua point, at Marriage for example, cause a loss in that life area?

Yes, a second door at any point in the room will cause an energy leak for that particular Life Situation.

Always strengthen the area near a second door with a Celestial Cure, whether an extra light, gold-fish, crystal, wind chime, green plant, or silk flowers. Try to sense what your room would prefer. You can tune into the Feng Shui of your own home better than anyone else. In this new era, when book knowl-edge is available to all, trust your own instincts rather than always relying on experts.

What other features should I beware of at various Ba-Gua points?

Once I received a letter from a melancholy bachelor in tropical Queensland, Australia. He lived in a large one-room apartment. Meeting women proved no trouble, but his relationships mysteriously fizzled out after a few dates. He put it down to his personal-ity. "I think I'm too casual and outspoken. Women don't like it." However, I thought his relaxed, honest attitude sounded pleasing, and I suspected bad Feng Shui.

The sketch he sent revealed the trouble—a small bar refrigerator at his I Ching Ba-Gua Marriage point. Astonishing as it sounds, the bar fridge froze his chances!

He moved the fridge fast. A year later he sent me his wedding photo. He and his new wife married on the beach wearing shorts, so his new wife evidently liked the casual life, too. The moral? Be careful where you place your fridge in a one-room apartment.

I notice Ba-Gua is spelled many ways in different books, from *Pa-Kua* to *Pah-Kwa*. Why is that?

When Chinese characters are transcribed into English, various different systems are used. Some systems spell certain sounds slightly differently.

Chapter Four

Harmonious Home & Workplace Locations

lucky & unlucky land shapes
money-magnet sites
neighbors & omens

Does the shape of our block of land matter?

Yes, greatly. In some countries, people will give away, or not use, odd little pieces or projections of land they own, rather than be stuck with an unlucky shape.

What are the luckiest shapes for blocks of land?

Regular shapes like squares and rectangles. A block with greater depth than width promotes family stability and it's better Feng Shui for wedge-shaped blocks to widen at the back.

When possible, choose a block with a higher rear area. This protects residents.

Which block of land shapes should I beware of?

If possible, avoid odd shapes where a piece seems missing, as in L shapes. Be wary of triangles, T shapes, or wedge-shaped blocks that narrow toward the back, indicating a lack of support. But if you already live on such a block, don't panic. Feng Shui is practical and usually offers a remedy.

Should I consider the overall shape of a large subdivision of land?

Yes. All the usual Feng Shui "shape" rules apply. If possible, buy your block of land in a subdivision with an even shape overall.

But if you lack a choice, and the subdivision is L- or knife-shaped (also called a "battle-axe" shape), it's luckier to buy your block in the controlling "handle" area, rather than the larger "blade" area, shown shaded.

Where on various shaped lots should a house be positioned for good Feng Shui? What are the cures for unlucky positions?

A central position facing the street at a straight angle is usually best, except for L-shaped blocks.

Residents of houses set at cross-angles often fight with neighbors unless a hedge, fountain, or flagpole is placed between the two houses.

Houses on triangular lots should not have a front door facing a triangle point. Cut off the triangle point with a line of flowers or green-ery, or place a round garden light near the point.

The illustration below shows the best site for houses on L-shaped blocks. Position a tall tree or garden lamp behind the house and grow flowers or

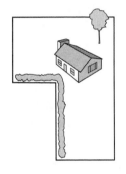

greenery along the two sides where marked.

With a T-shaped lot, an entrance in the base of the T boosts careers, but discourages study—house resi-dents will find friends unwilling to help when trouble arrives.

If the entrance is on top of the T, residents will suffer marriage and financial problems. The cure is to plant flowers or greenery along the two underside edges of the top bar of the T-shape, where illustrated. Locate your house where shown at right.

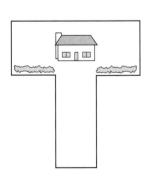

If your house is not posi-tioned centrally on your lot,

chapter 10 gives remedies for various imbalances that disturb the harmony of the four protective Feng Shui House Spirits.

What are the age-old Feng Shui rules for finding an auspicious or lucky site for a home?

Always trust your first impression of a place—the feeling you get when you initially see it. Locate a site you love passionately rather than make logical comparisons with a checklist.

Any other tips when looking for blocks of land?

Be wary of buying a block of land next to a vacant site—who knows what kind of neighbor you could get?

Don't buy near a dilapidated, unoccupied house, an electrical substation, high-tension wires, or a TV, radio, or mobile phone tower.

For harmony, it's best to buy in a residential area without a neighbor such as a school, church, cemetery, hospital, fire station, or funeral parlor. Common sense will tell you to avoid living near a rubbish dump!

It's also bad for your prosperity if you build a house with a front door opposite the gap between two much higher buildings—called a "slice cut out of the cake" in Feng Shui. In Western terms, you will suffer the effects of a wind-tunnel opposite.

Mmmmm . . . I like the sound of "money-magnet" sites. Quick—where do I find one?

A money-magnet site attracts the most prosperous currents of wind and water to you. In this peaceful environment, relationships flourish and so do careers. As a result, sooner or later (and usually sooner) the universe showers you with money.

A site halfway up a hill or slope, looking onto gently moving, not stagnant, water is considered wonderful Feng Shui. This is a true money-magnet position. Oddly enough, these places are exactly where the rich and famous build their fabulous villas. The mansions of film stars and millionaires on the Mediterranean provide a good example. Magnificent harborside homes in Sydney and Palm Beach also spring to mind.

A second money magnet site lies at the innermost point of an ocean or river bay, where water flows toward you, as illustrated in House A. Living at the outer part of the bay, or on a promontory,  does not attract such good Feng Shui. Here lots of money may pass through your hands, but you may not hang on to it (House B).

Is it lucky to live on top of a hill?

Surprisingly, it's not near as lucky as living halfway up a hill or slope. Living on top of a hill means it's hard to accumulate qi life energy—the wind disperses it too soon. This leaves you open to sudden reversals of fortune unless you add a grove of trees behind your house, to act as a protective Black Tortoise House Spirit (see page 131, on Protective House Spirits).

What other sites invite sudden reversals of fortune?

Other "reversal of fortune" sites include the top or bottom floors of a skyscraper, the tallest house in the street, or an exposed promontory.

Why is it bad Feng Shui to live opposite a T or Y intersection?

If you live opposite a T or Y intersection, unsettling energy from the road will hammer the home, tiring its

residents. This is one situation where you need to use a side door rather than the front door. A long-term solution is to grow a hedge of small bushy green shrubs between the road and your house, to block this disturbing energy. But don't place a large-trunk tree right opposite your front door. This creates further bad Feng Shui.

Another Celestial Cure? Place a small fountain between your home and the road, though this may prove costly. Some people prefer a round or octagonal red-backed Feng Shui mirror secured on the door frame above their door, to reflect back the troublesome energy. Make one by painting the back of an appropriate mirror red. Use an enlarging mirror for big problems.

Other special Ba-Gua mirrors, around four inches (or ten centimeters) in diameter, are often surrounded by eight special arrangements of black and white lines called trigrams. They are easy to buy in the East, or in the Chinatowns of a large city. Use these mirrors only on house exteriors.

As a final resort, build a high solid front fence, preferably painted white on the outside—a color rarely used in Feng Shui.

Our home lies at the end of a dead-end street. Is this good or bad Feng Shui?

It's bad Feng Shui. Residents in these houses will feel tired and suffer upsets and quarrels. While Westerners tend to see dead-end streets as peaceful, Eastern lore says the qi life energy, rushing down the street with no outlet, hammers the house or houses at the end of the street. The restless energy coming from car lights at night, as they turn at the end of the street, is called "tiger eyes."

The same remedies apply as in the previous question. In China, many houses have a little wall, called a *Ying Pei*, built just out from the front door, as a barrier to this type of sha qi or bad energy.

Why should I be cautious living near a school?

Feng Shui warns that unsettling energy accumulates near schools. Anyone living nearby (especially opposite) suffers from the overflow of problem energy. Quarrels, tiredness, emotional upsets, and headaches often result.

When possible, screen your view of the school. Keep thick coverings on windows looking on to schools and set up a physical barrier between your house and the school. Try a bushy green hedge, fountain, or high, solid fence out front.

When is it dangerous to live opposite or near a church?

Feng Shui warns that problem energy also accumulates near churches, especially those used more for funerals, memorial services, and unhappy occasions than joyous events like marriages and christenings. Those living nearby should apply the same remedies as for schools.

Oh dear! Our house looks onto a cemetery, which I hear is bad Feng Shui.

It's important to try and screen or block your view of the cemetery so house residents are not constantly gazing at a place of death. Excessive Yin energy also collects in cemeteries and this usually overflows to nearby houses, with unsettling results.

Often a lattice screen covered with flowers or vines outside your window provides a happy solution. But if all else fails, cover a window overlooking a cemetery with translucent blinds in sunshiny lemon or another cheery color.

A bridge or sharp freeway section points at our home. Is this bad Feng Shui?

Yes, and a sharp-edged bridge can also send sha qi, or bad energy. Try to block or screen the view, using any methods in the previous few answers. Again, a fountain between your house and the bridge will help improve the Feng Shui.

We have a view of a park in front of our house. How does this rate?

Park views are very good Feng Shui, especially in front of the house. They bring peace and harmony to those overlooking this green area. Later you will see how this space invites protection from the Red Bird, one of the four Feng Shui House Spirits.

Our home has water views. How can I use Feng Shui to double our prosperity?

Looking onto water, especially moving water, is very good Feng Shui for peace and prosperity. To double this lucky effect, hang a fairly large round or oval mirror on an interior wall, where it reflects the water views into your home.

Does a large electricity pole opposite our front door create bad energy?

Yes. Secure a small round or octagonal mirror (or a special Ba-Gua mirror from an Eastern market) above your front door frame to deflect the bad Feng Shui. If the pole opposite your door looks particularly ugly, an enlarging mirror creates a stronger effect.

A huge tree stands directly opposite our front door. How does this affect house residents?

Such a tree sends excessive Yin energy rushing into the house, through the front door. This overwhelms residents, causing quarrels and upsets. Consider removing the tree—such a position also makes it a danger should it fall on your house. (Don't forget to carry out the Feng Shui tree-cutting ritual in chapter 14 beforehand. See page 165.)

If removing the tree is not an option, secure a mirror above your door as in the previous answer, to reflect back the problem energy.

Another solution is to place a light on either side of your front door.

Our front window looks onto a large electrical tower or ugly chimney stack. What should I do?

As a short-term solution, try to screen the view from your house, perhaps with a vine or flower-covered lattice outside your window. Otherwise, consider keeping this window permanently screened with translucent drapes or pretty rice paper blinds.

In the long-term, try to create a barrier of bushy evergreen trees between your home and the electrical tower, remembering to avoid placing a large tree opposite your front door. A green hedge would be great, but may take ages to grow. Another option is to place a fountain in your garden between the ugly sight and your house.

Will I be happier in a street where house heights roughly match?

Yes, because this encourages qi life energy to flow more smoothly from house to house. Life in the neighborhood becomes more stable.

Neighboring houses are much higher than ours. How does this affect our Feng Shui?

Residents of taller houses will receive more qi life energy. As a result they will enjoy more good fortune. You could balance out the energy flow between houses by placing a flagpole as tall as your neighbor's house between the two houses. But consider extending your house to match the others.

We live in the tallest house in the area. How does this affect our Feng Shui?

You will receive more qi life energy than others nearby and hence receive more good fortune and opportunities. But you will also be more open than others to sudden reversals of fortune in all life situations.

Previous Residents

How will I benefit from knowing the fate of previous house residents?

The Chinese say, when moving into a house, you often repeat the destiny of previous residents. It's like wearing their shoes.

That's why you should enquire whether previous residents moved on to better things—perhaps a larger house in a better suburb. Or did they separate, go bankrupt, or move to a smaller home?

For this reason, houses bought at mortgagees' auction are not good Feng Shui. However, if you already live in a home where previous residents met an unhappy fate, do not panic. Knowledge is power and forewarned is forearmed. Just make sure you take extra care in the life area where the previous residents experienced trouble. Perhaps add a Celestial Cure at a suitable Ba-Gua point.

I recall a situation in New Zealand in which people discovered that long, long ago their farm was a Maori battleground. I realized why they were embroiled in a long-standing legal case and in constant friction with farmworkers.

We're moving into a newly built house. How does this rate?

You won't have so many past influences to counteract. But it will still pay to investigate the history of the site.

Our home is a former police station. What should we do?

Feng Shui advises against buying such a residence, as it retains lingering energy of grief and anxiety. If the house is in a coastal town or has water views, there's less need to worry. Otherwise, install a powerful Celestial Cure, such as two flutes, near the front entrance.

Neighbors

How do neighbors influence my destiny?

Like previous residents of your home, neighbors give an indication of the qi life energy of the area, and of your own fate.

What should I find out about my neighbors?

If you are inspecting an apartment or home you're hoping to move into, but see or hear quarreling neighbors, think twice. On the other hand, if smiling neighbors purr down the drive in a gleaming new car, this indicates a happy area with prosperous qi life energy.

Both my neighbors suddenly divorced. Should I be wary?

Previous answers show how your own fate often echoes your neighbors. Don't panic, but take action. Check with your partner regularly for any unresolved conflict. Keep communication open with frequent chats.

Most importantly, add a few Celestial Cures to your house—perhaps a fan in the Marriage area. You could also move your wedding photo to the Wisdom area.

Will I prosper if my neighbors suddenly win the lottery or become wealthy?

Hurrah! It's extremely likely. In some mysterious way, either through a job promotion or some unexpected bonus or windfall, you'll find new riches will appear in your own life. You'll be amazed.

To prosper, is it better to live in a small house in a wealthy area or a large house in a less expensive area?

By now you can probably see why it's better for your luck and wealth to buy a smaller home in a moneyed area than a large home in a rundown or less affluent area. Living in a wealthy area surrounds you with "prosperous qi." This rubs off on you.

Omens

What are Feng Shui omens? How can they help me?

An omen is a thing or event that hints at your future. Feng Shui says life contains no coincidences—every outer event connects with an inner meaning.

For example, if you are inspecting a house for sale, and a funeral hearse zips by in the traffic, or worse, stops outside even just to check tires, this is a bad omen for your happiness in this residence.

On the other hand, perhaps as you pull up outside, the radio suddenly plays your favorite song. To a person aware of omens, this would be a good sign.

Why should I beware blown lightbulbs, jammed doors, or any kind of door trouble?

These are traditional bad omens. If you're walking around inspecting a home and a lightbulb blows out, it's bad Feng Shui. Think twice about this home.

Door trouble of any kind is also bad Feng Shui. You may think it's coincidence that the door jams on an apartment you're inspecting, or you keep missing the agents with the keys. Feng Shui says otherwise.

We noticed a dead bird lying near a prospective home. Should we proceed?

No, this is another bad omen. If you've already purchased a home where this omen occurred, add a protective Celestial Cure to your home. A small fountain, bird bath, wind chime, or two flutes would be ideal.

I live in the country. Are there special omens to check?

Yes, and they relate to first impressions. When initially inspecting a likely home, take a quick look at

nearby hills, mountains, or the surroundings. Sometimes you'll get a fleeting impression that a nearby hill reminds you of something. What is it? A turtle, a smiling face, or a rat, as shown in the illustration just above the house roof.

Can you see it?

Ask yourself how you feel about the shape you see. It will be a good or bad omen according to your feelings.

When I first visited our new home, the hill behind reminded me of my favorite uncle's hat. What does this mean?

This is a good omen because it gave you a happy feeling. But another person might glance quickly at the hill and see an upturned boat—a traditional Feng Shui omen of bad luck. It indicates illnesses for daughters or prison sentences for sons.

Can the same omen be good Feng Shui for one person, and bad Feng Shui for another person?

Yes. For example someone who is a Rat in the Chinese zodiac (born 1924, 1936, 1948, 1960, 1972, 1984, 1996) would probably view a rat shape on a hill behind a prospective house as a good omen. To a farmer's wife (who sees rats as pests), it might be a bad omen.

My husband joked that the luxury blocks of apartments where we hope to live reminds him of filing cabinets. Is this a bad omen?

If your husband is an accountant or feels filing cabinets are pleasant objects, it's a good omen. But if you feel there's an unpleasant association or feeling of being filed away in an impersonal block, it's a bad omen.

Chapter Five

Happy Home & Workplace Designs

*lucky & unlucky house shapes
room layouts*

Do some building shapes encourage luck and harmony? What shapes should I beware of?

Even Winston Churchill said, "We shape our dwellings and afterwards our dwellings shape us."

Feng Shui wisdom reveals that regular building shapes like squares and rectangles bring good luck, as do the less common circles and octagons. Be wary of L, T, H, or U shapes—anything irregular.

Is it true a house with front and back doors in line causes money and luck to run out faster than they come in?

Yes, this is one of the most famous Feng Shui secrets.

You'll also find if you stand at anyone's front door and can see the back door, it creates an unpleasant feeling of being unwelcome. Unconsciously, you think about leaving.

What is the cure for front and back doors in line?

Stop qi life energy flowing straight in and out too fast. An easy way is to hang a wind chime inside the house, just in front of the back door. Another way is to block the line between front and back doors with a heavy solid item, like a wooden bookcase. A third option? Screen the back door, so that it's not visible to anyone entering from the front door.

What other problems can a central passageway cause?

This house design can cause residents to divide into two hostile camps. Conflict will deepen if children occupy bedrooms on one side, with the parental bedroom on the other side.

To fix this situation, place a wind chime at the end of the passage, or add a Celestial Cure like an extra light, midway along the passage. If friction is really bad, add a hardy green plant or two as well.

How can my U-shaped house disrupt family life?

Take care with a U-shaped home. Such a home can cause marriage problems for residents. This happens because rooms situated in the two protruding wings are regarded as "left out" of the main home area. The section between the wings is seen as a "missing heart."

A kitchen located in one of the wings will encourage the husband and children to eat out. Family life could disrupt, and the family may even break up.

Where should I position a master bedroom in a U-shaped house to prevent my partner spending nights elsewhere?

Try to position the master bedroom in the main body of the house, toward the back—not in the protruding wings.

Otherwise, Feng Shui warns the male partner can feel left out of the family and begin spending nights elsewhere.

Where possible, use the wings for rooms of lesser importance to the family, such as games rooms, guest rooms, extra bathrooms, sewing, TV, or hobby rooms.

Help! I'm stuck with an important room, like a kitchen or master bedroom, in a protruding wing.

Correct the bad Feng Shui by erecting a low hedge, decorative lattice fence, or line of flowers or shrubs where illustrated, to remake the house into a square or whole. Another cure is to "roof in" the empty middle section, making a covered patio underneath. You can also place two large mirrors on a back wall

of the main house where they reflect the protruding wing back into the main house.

What problems does an L-shaped house create?

The irregular shape implies something is "missing." As a result, residents can miss out on many opportunities.

What are the cures for an L-shaped house?

Place a tree, garden light, statue, or fountain in the garden diagonally opposite the L-shaped corner. This balances the shape and fixes the bad Feng Shui.

What is a "naughty nose" house?

This intriguingly named design is a T-shaped house with a protruding middle section—usually an entrance area.

Ancient Feng Shui manuscripts liken this to a jutting, or "naughty" nose. The "naughty nose" chokes the entrance of good qi life force energy into the house through the door or building mouth.

Result? Money or tiredness problems for residents.

How do I fix "naughty nose" money or energy problems?

Plant a bushy evergreen plant or tree either side of the "nose" as illustrated. For paved areas, use a potted shrub.

House Shape and Energy

How do house designs relate to the Chinese Five Elements?

The predominant shape of a house classifies it under one of the famous Chinese Five Elements: Fire, Earth, Metal, Water, or Wood.

Forget about the material from which your house is constructed—the shape is what counts.

What type of overall energy does my high-rise apartment have? Where is its power place?

A tall home such as a three-story dwelling, or apartment in a high-rise skyscraper, comes under the influence of the Wood element. Some Feng Shui writers also call this a "Spring house," to prevent confusion with the building material. House energy relates to creation, nourishment, and growth.

For good fortune in such a house, residents should place a green wooden item near the power place or focus area for beneficial energy: dining room, children's room, or bedroom.

What type of overall energy does my sharp-angled, pointy-roof house have? Where is its power place?

This shape house is called a "Fire house," as it's ruled by the Fire element. Your house energy relates to intellect and animal vitality. It is good Feng Shui for you to keep a red, pointed object, or an item made from leather, near the power place of the kitchen stove.

My house shape is a low ranch style with a flat roof. What type of energy does it have? Where is its power place?

A house shape such as yours is ruled by the Earth element. Overall, the energy of Earth homes is solid and enduring, but needs stimulation to prevent residents becoming set in their ways. For good Feng Shui, keep something yellow or made from clay or brick near your power place—anywhere associated with storage, such as your pantry, linen cupboard, or garage.

Our house shape is unusual—circular with curves and arches. What sort of energy does it have? Where is the power place?

This house shape comes under the influence of the Chinese Metal element, but it is often called an "Autumn house," to prevent people thinking such a building must be made of metal. For good Feng Shui, place a metal coin in power places—the study or kitchen.

Buildings with central domes fall under the Metal element, which relates to financial energy. This shape is rare in domestic buildings. More often you'll find banks, treasuries, and financial institutions intuitively settling in such a shape.

Our house is modern with lots of glass. What is its energy type? Where is its power place?

Your house is ruled by the Chinese Water element. Its energy relates to communication. Often stunningly complex and modern, Water houses frequently mix features of all other types. They can also result from extensions.

Power places center on water—bathroom, kitchen, sink, spa, or pool. For good luck, keep an item made of black glass near any of these areas.

Doorways and Destiny

What does my front door reveal about my destiny?

You may think your doors just hang there silently, but to a Feng Shui expert your doors speak volumes. Your front door can reveal secrets about your future, your finances, your health, and your happiness—even the number of arguments likely to take place in your home.

Discover a little Feng Shui door lore and you can increase your harmony and happiness!

What problems are caused by a front door that's too large?

It's like having a huge mouth in a face. Too much qi life energy rushes in, causing upsets, quarrels, and jittery dispositions.

What should I do about an overly large front door?

Hire a carpenter to reduce the size of the door, so that it looks correctly proportioned for the size of your home. If this proves too expensive or difficult, use the Eighth Celestial Cure—Heavy Objects.

Place two heavy statues (lions or dogs are popular) on either side of the front door to reduce the space available for qi life energy to enter. Bushy green shrubs here provide another option. Cumquat shrubs are ideal as their golden fruit invites money to your home.

Does a small front door cause bad Feng Shui?

Yes, in this case, it's like a tiny mouth on a face. Only a trickle of nourishing qi life energy enters. Eventually, residents become reserved, timid, or withdrawn. If you can't afford a bigger door, add mirror panels round the top and sides. Or you may prefer colored, stained-glass panels decorated with curving vines, cumquats, birds, or motifs of good omen.

We have two front doors. Does this matter?

Yes, it's like a face with two arguing mouths. This design encourages quarrels among residents. Close off one door, or make one door look more important with lamps either side and potted plants. Public buildings with this design suffer much staff friction.

Steps lead down to our front door from a road or stairway above. Does this affect our Feng Shui for better or worse?

Walking downward to reach your front door is bad Feng Shui—not good for the relationships or the careers of its residents.

Install a spotlight aimed at the roof of your house to increase the harmonious energy in your home. Another option is to position two door lights on either side of your front door. Switch them on as often as possible.

A third option? A garden light illuminating the path to your house—but this light must also shine on some area of your house to increase its harmonious energy. Yet another idea is to create one small artificial step going up, just outside your door threshold.

Is it okay to enter our home from the side garage?

Feng Shui views your house as a body. Entrance through the front door creates maximum harmony for residents.

Does it create problems to use our back door as our front door?

Yes. Muddled energy and instability result. Encourage all residents to use the front door, unless it faces a T or Y junction. In this last case, it's okay to use a side or back door.

Help! Our front door is smaller than our back door.

This means more energy will leave the house than enters, tiring the residents. Enlarge the front door with one of the cures given earlier.

What does my room layout, in relation to my front door, reveal about my fate?

The layout of rooms in a house influences the behavior and destiny of residents. The first room by the front door determines the atmosphere and character of the whole house.

What's the most auspicious or fortunate room to locate by the front door?

It's best that your front door opens into a well-lit, airy, spacious entrance foyer, without view of staircases, bedrooms, bathrooms, or kitchen. Unless there are special circumstance, a living room, sunroom, or family room is the best room to open off the entrance. This encourages a relaxed, balanced home life.

In a home without a separate entrance area, it's best if the front door opens into the living room.

Our entrance area is small, with a blank wall at the back and a side door opening to a corridor. Is this good or bad Feng Shui?

This situation is bad Feng Shui, especially for long-term house residents. Walking through the front door and coming up against a too-close wall causes problems with prosperity and personal qi life energy. Here's the remedy. Hang a mirror at eye level on the entrance back wall, so that those coming through the front door gain a feeling of space. If you like, place a green plant or flowers in front of the mirror on a small table or shelf.

The next best solution? Instead of the mirror, hang a landscape painting with some kind of perspective or feeling of distance.

Why is it dangerous to position a junk room, spare room, rumpus room, game room, or pool table room by the front door?

Because the first room by the front door determines the atmosphere of the home and influences behavior, a game room or pool table room here causes residents to waste their time. A rumpus room invokes quarrels due to its very name. Rename it, perhaps as a den, sunroom, "funroom," or whatever feels right.

A junk room by the front door causes the household to focus on the idea of junk each time they enter—not a harmonious influence. This setup also encourages accumulation of more junk.

My kitchen lies right next to the front door. Is this bad Feng Shui for dieters?

Yes. This layout encourages the household to nibble from dawn to dusk. Ideas for yummy snacks will constantly tempt you.

A kitchen minus a door worsens the problem so screen the door, add a bead curtain or new door. If your kitchen has a door, mirror the outside to reverse energy flow. (A mirror here also acts as a motivation tool.) As a last resort, hang a chime in the kitchen doorway.

Our laundry is the first room opening off the entrance . . .

Yours will tend to become a hard-work house. Never leave the laundry door open. If possible, mirror the outside of the laundry door, or hang a crystal in the doorway.

How does our guest powder room near the front door rate?

It may be fashionable, but it's bad Feng Shui! And never leave the door to the powder room open, it's terrible for your luck. Either mirror the outside of the powder-room door, hang a crystal in the doorway, or place a hardy green plant nearby.

How does a bedroom by the front door rate?

Sorry, but this common layout is not good Feng Shui. Worldly worries will linger on the minds of occupants. To enjoy the most refreshing sleep, move your bedroom as far from the front door as possible. If this is awkward, either mirror the outside of the bedroom door or hang a crystal near the doorway.

Staircases

What are the most fortunate positions for staircases?

Position staircases so they are out of sight when the front door is opened. Tucked away toward the side of the house is a reasonable location.

What are the unluckiest positions and shapes for staircases?

A staircase opening right by the front door is bad Feng Shui. Chinese people avoid this feature as qi life energy travels too quickly upstairs, without a chance to flow evenly round the ground floor. Money and opportunities then roll out of the house too fast.

There are many cures. Hang a wind chime between the first stair and the entrance, install a bright light above the staircase, place a round mirror on the landing, or a green plant underneath the stairs.

It's also better if the staircase has a landing or changes direction halfway up, with the staircase front curving away rather than starting in a straight line facing the front door. Individual stairs need risers. Blank spaces between steps let qi energy slip through.

Which is luckier, odd or even number of staircase steps?

A staircase with an odd number of stairs is luckier. Many Chinese will even add an extra step, to improve their fortunes.

Why does Feng Shui avoid spiral staircases?

Their shape sends qi life energy whirling in a dangerous corkscrew motion, which causes upsets and quarrels. A central spiral staircase is worst because it "bores into" the heart of the house. Fix the problem with a twenty-four-hour light at the top of the spiral staircase.

Hallways

How should hallways and corridors be constructed?

They should be wide and well lit. Long, narrow corridors cause many Feng Shui problems. At the very least, hang a wind chime halfway along a problem corridor, or place hardy green plants or mirrors at intervals. Do not hang two mirrors opposite each other, as energy will bounce back and forth. It's best if doors to rooms on either side of the corridor are not exactly opposite each other. If they are, place a green plant near one door in the corridor.

I'm warned I occupy a "Dragon's Mouth" room. Is there a remedy?

Any room at the end of a long narrow corridor is said "to peer into the Dragon's Mouth." It's as dangerous as it sounds! Qi life energy rushes along the corridor too quickly, hammering the end room with disturbing energy. This causes many difficulties for occupants.

The remedy? Either place a screen around the door to stop qi life energy hurtling straight in, or place large green plants on either side of the door. A wind chime or crystal in the doorway is the third option.

Window Wisdom

Our house contains many windows. Can this make our children bad-mannered smart alecks?

Yes. Feng Shui usually views the house as a body and windows as eyes. But when comparing the ratio of doors to windows, doors represent parental mouths and windows represents the mouths of children. Too many windows mean too many yabbering children's mouths, resulting in family arguments.

When windows outdo doors in size (and this happens in most Western homes) Feng Shui warns that children will ignore parental advice and not respect their elders. (In this situation, large windows with small panes count as one window.)

What is the correct Feng Shui door-to-window ratio?

Windows, or children's mouths, should not outnumber doors or parental mouths by more than three to one. To harmonize relations in a multiwindow home, hang a small silver bell or wind chime, preferably made from tiny bells, near your front door. Every time the door opens the bell tinkles and the windows (children) are forced to listen to this parental voice.

The sound of a bell is always good Feng Shui. Many cultures worldwide ascribe special magic and power to its ring.

Our lounge room features large matching windows at either end. Why does this unsettle people?

Qi life force energy flows too quickly through the room and out these windows. As a result, room occupants feel unsettled and jittery. Make one window the focal point, perhaps with special drapes hung alongside the window to make it look larger. Partly cover the other window with drapes to make it seem smaller. Occupants of the room will now feel more calm and comfortable.

Is it bad Feng Shui to leave a broken window unmended?

Yes. Feng Shui warns never to leave broken windows, even when unnoticeable. They invite eye trouble.

What's best, windows that slide up and down, or open out or in?

Outward opening windows invite better Feng Shui because the body movement opening them expands your personal qi life energy field. Inward opening windows are harmful to house residents. Eventually residents will tend to become timid.

Our windows are fixed to slide only halfway up. What does this mean?

Tradition says that people living in homes with these windows enjoy giving others false impressions.

We live in an older-style house with narrow windows. How does this affect our Feng Shui?

Narrow windows can restrict opportunities for house residents and cause their mental outlook to narrow, too.

How is Feng Shui affected by circular, semicircular, arched, or octagonal windows?

These shapes invite harmonious energy into your house.

Are bay windows good Feng Shui?

Yes. The shape of a bay window resembles a partial Ba-Gua or octagon. So they are very lucky indeed. When they look onto water, as well, you have a most auspicious nook in your home. Make this spot into a delightful haven with window seats where you can curl up with a book and enjoy yourself.

How do split-level floors affect residents?

The Chinese say differing floor levels can cause ups and downs in the life of residents. Locate eating or dining areas on higher sections for better Feng Shui. Extra lights on the lower section will increase harmonious qi life energy.

Why are exposed beams bad Feng Shui?

Many Western architects favor exposed beams. But they are bad Feng Shui and create disturbing currents in the qi life energy of a room. They compress qi, causing tension, headaches, or quarrels for those sitting or sleeping beneath.

What are the cures for exposed beams?

The traditional Chinese cure is to lower the ceiling so the beams are invisible, or to hang a silky red tassel from each beam. However, Westerners who prefer an unobtrusive cure can place clear quartz crystals on top of the beams—as many as you feel the room needs. A small room may need a few, a large room, more. Two flutes along the beams make fine cures, too.

How else can I remedy exposed beams in a bedroom?

To prevent headaches, quarrels, and other upsets, apply one or other of the cures in the previous answer. Try to ensure the beams do not cross your bed, but run parallel with it.

Sleeping in a four-poster bed with a solid canopy also protects you from the bad effects of the beams.

What about exposed beams in a kitchen or dining room?

Avoid a table directly under a beam—this will cause friction while eating. If your table is rectangular, it's best the beam does not cross the table, but runs parallel with it. Even then, you need to add another Celestial Cure like a chandelier or candles, because of the rectangular table shape, which is not good Feng Shui either.

Is a skylight good Feng Shui?

Yes. Increasing the amount of light adds harmonious, healing energy to your home. Circular, oval, or octagonal skylights are best. The latest octagonal skylights feature added electric lighting, for nighttime use, and timber trims to enhance period homes.

Are very sharply sloping ceilings good or bad Feng Shui?

They are bad Feng Shui. If you sleep in such a room, or an attic, hang a wind chime at the lowest point of the sloping ceiling. This disperses the qi life energy that accumulates there.

Are there Feng Shui guidelines on garages?

Yes. When possible keep them in the same line as the rest of the house, rather than jutting out at right angles with a huge door that dwarfs the front door of your home.

For instance, with a ranch-style home, it's better if the garage is at either end and painted to match the house.

Residents in homes where garages jut out at right angles will suffer more from stress.

Chapter Six

Good Feng Shui, Room by Room

kitchen, bathroom & bedroom bliss

Food for thought—what's the most important item to check in your kitchen?

In all of Feng Shui, only the position of your bed matters more than the position of your humble kitchen stove. Feng Shui wisdom says a badly placed stove can cause a chain reaction of either peevishness or peace to run right through your home. Eventually this affects your family's health and money, too.

What is the "Peevish Cook" position? Why is it so bad?

This recipe for disaster occurs when the person cooking stands at the stove, facing away from the kitchen door or doors.

Feng Shui says it's very important that a cook is never startled and can easily see anyone entering the door. Centuries-old manuscripts explain that the qi life energy of the kitchen and cook should always remain smooth and unruffled.

Anyone who enters unexpectedly jars the personal qi energy field of the cook, as well as that of the room. The cook then becomes peevish.

The sha qi, or discord, transfers to the food and then to those who eat it. Eventually the disposition and performance of everyone in the house deteriorates.

What is the "Peaceful Cook" position?

This occurs when anyone cooking faces the main kitchen door so they can easily see anyone entering. Unfortunately, I find in most Western countries only rarely is a kitchen stove correctly placed. Island-bench and motor-home stoves are usually better positioned.

Any restaurant owner will tell you that a happy chef generally creates a happy restaurant, while a cranky chef creates a restaurant where unhappiness reigns.

Can you demonstrate the effects of the Peevish Cook position?

Imagine a mother carefully stirring a tricky sauce at the stove, with her back to the door. At the crucial moment for the sauce, her teenage son tiptoes in and puts his arms round her waist. "Guess what, Mum? I'm home from school early. What's to eat?"

The mother is startled and surprised, and the sauce spoils slightly. Later at the table, her husband murmurs that his favorite sauce tasted a bit peculiar and the wife feels a touch resentful. The atmosphere at the table becomes niggling, the kids get cranky, and later argue about doing their homework.

Suddenly fed up, the husband watches TV instead of finishing an overdue work report. Next day his boss asks for the report. Goodbye pay raise! Goodbye overseas holidays. Yet who would think to blame the position of the kitchen stove?

What is the cure for the Peevish Cook position?

It's simple. Hang a wind chime or crystal between the stove and kitchen door, or doors. This corrects the qi life energy flow.

Is there another cure for my unlucky stove position?

Another traditional cure is to mirror the wall area behind or around the stove, so that the cook can see the kitchen door or doors while cooking. This looks quite smart in a kitchen, although to Western eyes it looks strange. Reflective tiles, perhaps in burnished metal, may be more acceptable.

What part of the kitchen stove predicts family wealth?

The number of burners on your stovetop reveals all. The more burners, the wealthier you will become! Feng Shui says there's an intimate connection between your stove, food, and wealth—this even reflects in the Chinese words for food and wealth.

How do stovetop burners increase or decrease my money?

Feng Shui says it's important to rotate use of your stovetop burners. Leaving some burners unused blocks household money flow.

Yuk. I hate cleaning the stove. But is it true an unclean stove reduces my prosperity?

Yes. Feng Shui says grime on your stove clogs channels for future wealth.

I've delayed mending my broken stove, and am making do with a microwave. How does this affect family Feng Shui?

Very badly. Fix your stove as soon as possible. A broken, unused stove invites many Feng Shui problems.

Why is a poorly lit kitchen unlucky?

A dark kitchen lacks harmony and transfers gloom to everyone in the house. Add an extra light to improve the Feng Shui.

I was given an expensive set of kitchen knives as a wedding gift. Does it invite trouble to display them?

Yes! Constantly gazing at instruments of strife invites turmoil to your house. Keep the knives out of sight.

Our kitchen looks onto an ugly bare wall. What now?

Looking onto an ugly wall brings you up against a financial and emotional wall and eventually causes all kinds of upsets in the home. Grow flowers or green vines up the walls—you may need to add a trellis. If you rent, potted climbing plants provide another option.

A third option? Ask an artistic friend to paint an attractive wall mural of flowers and vines, or any nature-based theme.

Our kitchen overlooks a tranquil park. Is this good Feng Shui?

Yes, this brings good energy to all who use the kitchen.

Bathroom Bliss

Is a centrally located bathroom good or bad Feng Shui?

It's bad Feng Shui unless you add mirrors to the internal bathroom walls. Try to locate bathrooms away from the front door, to the side or back of your house.

I'm told the wrong lavatory position flushes away money luck. Do I have an "unlucky loo"?

A lavatory visible immediately as you open the bathroom door brings the worst possible Feng Shui. It flushes away your money luck.

Old manuscripts explain that as a bathroom is a place where water (symbolic of money) enters and leaves your house, the bathroom layout affects residents' internal plumbing and money. It's best your lavatory is housed in a small separate room. And keep the toilet lid down.

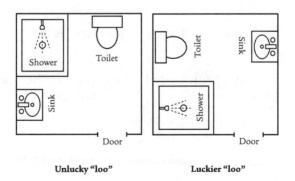

Unlucky "loo"   Luckier "loo"

How do I fix my "unlucky loo"?

You could screen your lavatory behind a smoked glass or other enclosure, so it's not immediately visible when opening the bathroom door. Short of cash or renting? Two lacquered bamboo blinds make an inexpensive screen.

Otherwise, hang a sparkling clear quartz crystal near the bathroom door to improve energy flow. Or you could mirror the outside of the bathroom door, making sure this mirror does not cut off the head of the tallest person in the house. Another option? Add a plant near or in front of the bathroom door.

Is an en suite bathroom good Feng Shui?

Modern architects say, "Yes," to the en suite bathroom, but ancient Chinese wisdom says, "No!" That's because a bathroom facing a bedroom emits bad qi, inviting problems with residents' digestive tracts. The cure? A crystal placed between bath and bed, or a mirror on the bathroom door. Always keep the door closed to an en suite bathroom.

Is our walk-in wardrobe between en suite bathroom and bedroom good or bad Feng Shui?

It's excellent Feng Shui, preventing the need for a special cure, as discussed previously.

What is the effect of a small bathroom with a large door?

This is not good Feng Shui. It encourages house residents to spend excessive amounts of time in the bathroom primping and preening. Remedy by hanging a mirror or favorite picture on the wall opposite the bathroom door.

Do spas, whirlpools, and bubbling jets affect bathrooms?

Any bubbling water device brings good Feng Shui and extra energy to household residents.

What are the best bathroom colors for harmony and peace?

Pale pastel wall colors like peach, apricot, lemon, blue, lavender, and green add harmony in the bathroom. Avoid the energy-draining effect of all white. But if you're stuck with white, add cheery splashes of bright color in towels, shower curtain, or bath mats.

Why are creamy pearl colors lucky in bathrooms?

The bathroom is ruled by the mighty Water Dragon, who loves the soft, creamy color of pearls. Legend says dragons actually dine on nothing but cream-colored ocean pearls.

Why is a tortoise-shell pattern good for bathroom accessories?

The Black Tortoise is one of the four protective House Spirits of Feng Shui. (More about these later.) Therefore, anything associated with a tortoise brings extra good Feng Shui. The tortoise-shell pattern adds interest in towel rails, soap cases, and other items.

What fragrances and bath oils have good Feng Shui?

Jasmine, mandarin, orange, magnolia, and peach oil are preferred. If you want to add scent to gift wrap paper, dab a few drops of oil on cotton wool and leave overnight with the gift wrap in a sealed bag. Also, a little oil dabbed onto a lightbulb spreads delicious fragrance through a room in a most delightful way.

Wake Up to Good Bedroom Energy

What is the most fortunate bedroom location?

To enjoy calmer, more refreshing sleep, locate your bedrooms as far from the front door as possible at the back of the house or upstairs, at the rear. Feng Shui says this means worldly worries will intrude less on your sleep.

Should I consider compass directions, when positioning beds?

It's not necessary. International Dragon Door Feng Shui says the existing position of your main bedroom door determines where your bed should go. And most problem positions can be corrected with mirrors or crystals. (Doors are a central focus in many mystical and philosophic traditions.)

What is the Cure for a bedroom located right by the door?

The traditional and most effective Feng Shui cure is to mirror the outside of your bedroom door. This changes the qi life energy flow near your front door.

However, mirroring the door may prove difficult. It's not acceptable sometimes in Western houses. Your second best option is to hang another Celestial Cure, such as a crystal, in your bedroom doorway, or close by. A sparkling clear quartz crystal is ideal. Many bookshops and New Age shops sell these from $10 upward, ready to hang on a ribbon.

How do I find the most favorable Emperor bed position?

Move your bed so it's diagonally opposite your main bedroom door, as shown in the illustration. This gives you a commanding view of the room while in bed and makes it difficult for anyone to enter the room without first being seen by you. Feng Shui says unexpected entrances cause qi life energy fields to disrupt into jagged patterns that gradually create disharmony.

Sleeping in the Emperor position revitalizes you, as the qi life energy of both your body and the room remain smooth and tranquil.

What is the—shudder—"Coffin" position? It even sounds scary!

Beware of the Coffin Position, which occurs when you sleep opposite the doorway with your feet pointing directly toward the door gap.

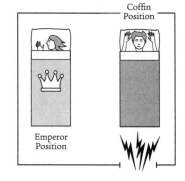

Why is it called the Coffin position?

In the East, this is the position in which corpses were wheeled from the room, feet first.

Can the Coffin position shorten your life up to four years?

Many Eastern Feng Shui masters warn that this is so.

Help! My bedroom is so tiny I'm forced into the Coffin position.

Hang a wind chime or crystal between your feet and the door to correct the energy flow. Many people prefer crystals for this situation because they throw beautiful rainbow lights when sunlight shines.

Do windows behind my bed's headboard affect me for better or worse?

Windows behind your bed weaken your personal qi life energy field, and your subconscious stays on alert while you sleep. The result? Less refreshing sleep.

For comfort and security, plus better quality sleep, keep a solid, straight wall behind your bedstead. Subconsciously, you'll relax more while you sleep, and awaken revitalized.

Is it better Feng Shui to sleep in a double or single bed?

Feng Shui reveals that the physical gap that occurs when partners sleep in twin beds will, over time, create an emotional gap. Double beds are better.

What can I do about serious quarrels in the bedroom?

Unless you sleep in the most favorable Emperor position, try moving your bed to a different spot. Or add a sparkling crystal in the window, where it will throw rainbow lights. An attractive extra lamp with a peach or pink shade will increase harmonious energy, too.

My bed position is neither good (the Emperor position) nor bad (the Coffin position). How do I improve it?

Hang a mirror, as illustrated, to reflect the entrance within your line of vision when in bed. This is a very important Feng Shui principle. If you can't see the doorway when lying in bed, then, among other problems, unexpected entrances will startle you, causing room and personal qi energy to disrupt into jagged, inharmonious lines.

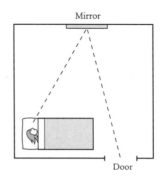

This sets up a field of discord around you.

My partner insists our bed run on a north-south line. But the way he has positioned it is bad Feng Shui—we can't see the door when in bed. What can I do? I hate fights!

Relax. Feng Shui is wonderfully practical. As in the previous answer, hang a mirror so you can see the main bedroom door when in bed.

Why do some Feng Shui experts dislike bedroom mirrors?

Certain Eastern cultures believe that at night the soul departs the body. When returning to the body before wake-up time, it's said the soul can receive a shock when it sees itself in a mirror.

However, Western culture is happy with mirrors in bedrooms—they are a tradition. Unless you personally feel uneasy about mirrors, you can use them to solve many problems. Listen to your own intuition to decide. No outside expert knows your house and its moods as well as you.

What color bedsheets encourage romance for single women?

Pink or peach sheets radiate romantic energy and whisper to the cosmos you're looking for love. The next best colors for bedroom harmony are pale pastels, or nature prints such as flowers and leaves.

My child's bedroom is vacant due to overseas travel . . .

Hang a mirror on the wall opposite the unused door. This encourages a safe return to the house.

Does a crack in bedroom plaster mean anything?

Quick! Send for a plasterer. Feng Shui says this heralds a cracked relationship for those in the bedroom.

Any good luck tips for my new bedroom in a new house?

Buy a new bed and mattress to encourage a fresh start and fresh luck. Or at least buy a new set of matched sheets in a color or pattern with good Feng Shui. This starts you on a new and better cycle of good fortune.

Restrict electrical items in your bedroom. Feng Shui warns against a bedroom crammed with television, radio, electric alarm clock, electric blanket, mobile phone, and other items. They create disruptive energy fields, which discourage sleep.

What is good Feng Shui for the bedroom of anyone very seriously ill?

Hang a painting, photo, or print of a peach tree or peach blossom near their bed, in their line of vision. The ancient Chinese say this will help the person get better, cheer them, and brighten their personal qi life energy field. If you give an invalid a gift of this sort of artwork, explain to them why it is good Feng Shui.

Chapter Seven

Good Feng Shui,
Room by Room (Continued)

seating secrets
living & dining rooms
studies, nurseries & other rooms

What is the Dragon seat of power?

It's the most influential seat in a room. Whoever sits here gains extra energy and a power advantage over others in the room.

When sitting in a Dragon seat, your personal qi energy field is not jarred by unexpected entrances.

How do I find the Dragon seat of power in a room?

It's always a seat facing the door but as far away from it as possible, preferably not in a direct line but diagonally. When there are several doors in

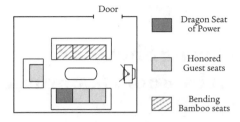

a room, the Dragon seat (or seats) gives the most commanding view of these, enabling sight of anyone entering or leaving.

What are Honored Guest seats? How do they affect occupants?

Honored Guest seats are secondary power seats, often quite near Dragon seats. They also give the occupant a good view of the door. You might decide to seat someone here you like, perhaps a favorite uncle.

What is a Bending Bamboo position? Who should sit here?

The remaining seats, with poor view of the door, or back to the door, are known as Bending Bamboo seats. Anyone sitting here bends like a bamboo in the wind to the stronger forces of the Dragon and Honored Guest seats. These are ideal places to seat someone like a nosey or unwanted visitor.

Is it best to always seat people according to these power rules?

It's important that you at least understand the forces at work. Then you can experiment and have fun. You might decide to put an overbearing salesman into the weaker power position of a Bending Bamboo seat. But if you're a shy teenager who has invited a date to your house for the first time, you might put yourself into an Honored Guest seat for confidence and place your nervous guest into the Dragon seat.

Of course, a Dragon seat of power will not turn a withdrawn person into a blabbermouth, nor will a Bending Bamboo seat turn a gasbag into a considerate conversationalist. But why not use every advantage you can? Knowledge is power, too.

My children sometimes sneak into a Dragon seat. Will this affect them?

Use common sense. If young children are already rebellious, don't let them watch TV late at night sitting in power seats. You may never get them to bed.

How should I position our L-shaped seating unit to avoid "poison arrows"?

Don't position the arrow-shaped corner of your seating unit to point toward a nearby bed in a bedroom, or as shown in the illustration. This sends bad energy, or "poison arrows" toward bed occupants, disturbing their sleep. It's often safer to position the unit along two back walls.

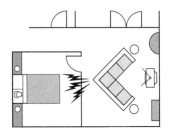

What style furniture creates a relaxed atmosphere and good Feng Shui?

Where possible, choose furniture with curved or rounded shapes rather than hard, sharp angles. The latter is more suited to an office.

Any other helpful seating tips?

If you are a lonely single person, don't group chairs in the lonely, odd numbers like one, three, or five. Go for even numbers to encourage company. As the Chinese proverb says, "Happiness comes in pairs."

What is a harmonious shape for a living room?

A square or rectangle is best, but a rarely found circle or octagon is also good Feng Shui.

Why do L-shaped living rooms often cause problems?

This shape means one section of the Ba-Gua will be missing. As a result, residents often miss out on opportunities related to the particular missing area of the Ba-Gua.

How do I fix Feng Shui problems in an L-shaped living room?

One easy way is to hang a mirror (preferably round or oval) to visually extend the missing area and symbolically make the shape whole. The illustration at the end of chapter 3 shows how. You can also hang a crystal where shown, or use a screen to divide the room into two square rooms.

Will a door at the Prosperity area drain away my money?

Yes. Some people lock any door at this point. But if you have to use it, add a Celestial Cure nearby, such as a wind chime, crystal, plant, extra light, or goldfish.

I live in a one-room apartment with a mini-fridge at my Prosperity area. Is this bad Feng Shui?

Yes. Strange as it sounds, this can "freeze" your prosperity. Many people have told me of their improved prosperity after moving the fridge and adding a Celestial Cure.

My piano sits at the Prosperity area. Is this good Feng Shui?

Yes! A piano brings delightful Feng Shui and harmony anywhere, while a grand piano is even grander. One former financial struggler, a single mother with two children, confided how she moved her piano to the Prosperity area, then sat there once a day playing and singing the song "Money, Money, Money." About two weeks later, she found a job after being out of work for eight months.

What else should I avoid at the Prosperity area of a living room?

Tradition warns against placing an electric kettle or coffeemaker here. The steam discourages the energy of money.

I hear fireplaces can cause trouble. What is the remedy?

Wherever an open fireplace with chimney is located in a room, an energy leak results at this actual point of the Ba-Gua. A mirror above the mantelpiece is a common remedy.

Where should I place my television to increase harmonious energy?

A TV stirs up the qi life energy in a room wherever it is placed. Decide which life situation of the Ba-Gua you would like activated and place the TV at this spot. For instance, if you're a student who has registered for part-time work acting in TV commercials, you might like to keep your TV at the Fame position of the Ba-Gua—the middle of the wall opposite your main living room door.

Dining Rooms

What are favorable shapes for dining tables and other tables?

Round, oval, and octagonal table shapes (the latter is known in the East as an "Eight Immortals" table) encourage harmony. It's no accident that tense political meetings often take place at a round or oval table, to reduce friction.

When possible, use small round or oval tables for wedding receptions. King Arthur sure knew what he was doing when he sat his knights at a round table!

What table shapes should I avoid?

Rectangular tables create bad Feng Shui as they increase conflict—the longer the sides, the greater the conflict. No wonder wedding guests often argue after hours sitting at tables like this. Six-sided tables are bad Feng Shui, too, especially when they feature slightly rounded or missing corners.

Does the number of diners affect table harmony?

Yes. Two to four people can eat harmoniously at a square table. But if three people—say, parents and a child—always eat at a square table, then long-term problems can result. For instance, one parent and the child may tend to always side against the other parent.

Is a chandelier good Feng Shui?

Yes, because it combines crystals and lights.

Why is a mirror in the dining room a happy idea?

A mirror adds prosperity to the diners, especially when it is positioned to "double" the food and reflect images of abundance.

Ensure that the mirror does not reflect the door of any nearby toilet.

Why are exposed beams dangerous in dining rooms?

Exposed beams are always bad Feng Shui as they compress qi life energy. If you can, lower the ceiling to cover them. Otherwise hang a Celestial Cure, such as a red tassel, flute, or crystal.

In a dining room, avoid placing a table under beams as they cause stress and quarrels. With a rectangular table, at least position the table to run parallel with the beams rather than let a beam chop a table in two. Brides holding receptions in Old World settings need to be wary of these beams, too. Switch on any chandeliers nearby.

Nurseries

Where is the most fortunate location for a baby's room?

Common sense says place it near the parents' room, and Feng Shui says keep both rooms toward the back of the house. Then worldly troubles intrude less on sleep.

Where is the best spot for a baby's cot?

At the I Ching Children point of the Ba-Gua—midway along the wall to the right of the nursery door. However, use common sense. If your door lies at the extreme end of the wall in the Helpful People position, the cot may then be too near the door. In this case, move the cot further from the door, 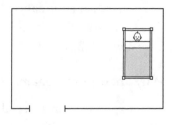 with a solid wall rather than weakening windows behind the head of the cot.

A heavy cupboard already sits in the Ba-Gua Children spot . . .

It's always good Feng Shui to place a yellow or white item at this position—maybe a nursery nightlight or soft toy.

Any tips to increase family harmony when furnishing our nursery?

It's important that the nursery contains not just the separate qi life energy of mother and baby, but a harmonious mingling of the whole family's energy.

Achieve this by ensuring all family members help decorate the nursery. Perhaps dad could make a toy box, while older brothers and sisters paint a simple bright wall picture or choose new wall colors.

This also helps older children accept the new baby into the family more easily.

I need nursery decor themes with good Feng Shui.

Why not use your baby's special moonlight (Yin) or daylight (Yang) lucky charms in room decor? Check the chart in chapter 16 to find these.

Use you imagination. For instance, if your baby is born in a Rabbit year, the official lucky charms are a cat and boat. Your nursery could feature a border of cute cats marching around the wall, or cat motifs on blankets. An older brother or sister might draw a boat rowed by a rabbit and cat as a wall picture.

As your Rabbit child gets older, a handyman father might easily convert the bed into the base of a fun boat. Use a sheet or mosquito net as a sail.

Study Rooms

Where is the most fortunate location for a formal study room?

Use common sense. If you are worried that your children don't study enough, position the study by the front door. This will help keep study on their minds. With overstudious children, position the study away from your front door.

Where should a student desk be placed in a bedroom?

Place it so the occupant faces the door, but sits as far from it as possible, preferably in a diagonal line. This constitutes a Dragon desk of power.

My desk is fixed against a wall so I can't see the door. What now?

Hang a mirror on the wall, so you can see the door. Otherwise you can still improve the Feng Shui to some degree by keeping a small round mirror (at least as large as a powder compact) in your desk drawer. Add a green plant or a crystal paperweight to your desk as well.

I study at the kitchen table and sometimes at the dining room table. Does this matter?

Yes. It's best to work in one place, as study qi then accumulates in this spot—a study atmosphere that makes concentrating easier. To further improve creativity and flow, add a print or painting of a water view to your study. A "water wheel" theme is ideal Feng Shui here. A globe of the world at the Ba-Gua Wisdom area in a study or bedroom is another often-used Feng Shui device to help students.

I can't study in our home. What can I do?

Move to your local library as such a place already has study qi or study energy. Also, you won't be so tempted to jump up and down for coffee, or make phone calls and chat.

I take formal exams soon. The exams will be held in a building I've never visited. Any success tips?

If you're nervous, visit the examination building at least a week before the event. The ancient Chinese Art of Placement says contemplating an unknown place creates strain. You'll feel more relaxed on your second visit, at exam time.

Hobby Rooms

Why is a hobby room, or hobby display, good Feng Shui?

You indulge in a hobby for pure delight, so a hobby room adds harmonious energy to the household. The only exception is a hobby related to conflict, such as war games, collecting antique pistols, or hunting knives. A display of any kind of war instruments creates very bad Feng Shui. If you must, keep these items in a room at the back of the house.

Where should a hobby room be located?

Most hobby rooms add harmonious energy and character to a home and please visitors, too. So why not place them prominently? The nearer your hobby room lies to the front door, the more prominence your hobby will achieve in your life.

Rooms to Beware Of

How does Feng Shui rate game rooms?

Game rooms are best located toward the back of your home. A billiard room, for instance, right by the front door, will gradually change the house atmosphere and cause residents to fritter time.

However, a game room for the children is good Feng Shui, as long as it's kept a reasonable distance from the front door.

Why is a junk room dangerous?

A junk room in your home is very bad Feng Shui. And if it's right by the front door, it's extremely bad Feng Shui, tiring residents and downgrading their health and welfare. Every time anyone goes in or out they unconsciously focus on the thought of junk. This attracts more junk, and the overall effect is negative.

If you have a junk room, set aside a few weekends to clear the mess. Give away anything unwanted. Hoarding things for a rainy day is bad Feng Shui. As soon as you've emptied the room you'll feel a burst of refreshing energy and uplifted spirits.

Hurry! Turn your junk room into a room for enjoying music, TV viewing, study, or hobby activities.

Why should I rename a rumpus room?

Rumpus is another name for quarrel or conflict, and Feng Shui says "Like attracts like." Rename the room a sunroom, funroom, den, or whatever appeals to you.

My granny says an unused room sulks. Is this similar to bad Feng Shui?

Yes. Feng Shui says unused rooms develop bad energy and attract misfortune. It amounts to the same thing. Agree on a new use for the room.

Chapter Eight

Transform Your Apartment's Energy

increasing luck while renting

What lucky influences should I seek in an apartment building site?

Get wise and apply the previous Feng Shui location and design guidelines from chapters 4 and 5. For instance, it's best if your apartment building is roughly the same height as your neighbors rather than dominating the cityscape, or being dwarfed by other buildings.

Take a bow if your apartment looks onto moving water, sits halfway up a gently sloping hill, or seems to harmonize with its surroundings. Check views, neighbors, and surrounding influences—all the usual factors.

Watch that a nearby building does not sit at a cross angle to yours, with a sharp edge pointing toward your building emitting "poison arrows," or bad energy. Don't buy in a block opposite a T- or Y-road intersection. And remember, if your individual apartment lies at the end of a long narrow corridor, you are "peering into the Dragon's mouth." Apply a Celestial Cure, such as a plant, near the door.

Should I consider the overall shape of an apartment block as well as my individual home within?

Yes. It's better if your building is an even, balanced shape, such as a square, circle, or rectangle, or a mix of these.

What high-rise block shapes should I avoid?

Beware of buildings with triangular tops. Buildings shaped like an L or T, or anything with "missing

sections" cause Feng Shui problems.

The Chinese also avoid H-shaped buildings because the shape attracts tough times for occupants. In an L-shaped or "battle axe" building, you'll have better

luck living in an apartment in the controlling handle area, rather than the larger "blade" section, shown darker in the figure.

How do curved balconies rate on an apartment block?

They invite good Feng Shui, and help harmonize many problems.

Does the ancient lore on the position of the Green Dragon, White Tiger, Black Tortoise, and Red Bird apply in the city?

Yes. Where possible, choose an apartment block with a clear outlook or a park, gardens, or much lower building in front. This gives space for the Red Bird Feng Shui House Spirit to fly. Taller buildings behind give the symbolic protection of the Black Tortoise, with its hardy shell. To please the Green Dragon, buildings to your left as you look out from the entrance should be lower than buildings behind. To invite White Tiger influences, buildings to your right (as you stand looking out from the entrance) should be lower than buildings to your left.

For easy recall, think of this ideal setup as a protective "lucky horseshoe" hugging your building.

How do taller buildings near my apartment affect me?

Tallest buildings should be behind you for protection. Avoid living in a smaller building sandwiched between two taller buildings.

Feng Shui likens this situation to a child between two greedy bullies—the taller buildings suck energy away.

Is it wise to pay more for water views in front?

Yes, it helps you prosper. Where possible, hang a mirror to reflect the water views inside. Fountains or artificial pools in front of your block are great, too, but water behind your home is not so favorable. Water behind means you may see opportunities, but be unable to benefit from them.

Will the common drive and entrance of my apartment building affect my wealth, energy, and well-being?

Yes, check them out. The ideal driveway to attract money is wide, curving, and either semicircular or circular. A well lit, spacious entrance, with stairs or elevators not immediately visible but tucked away to the side or elsewhere, brings good Feng Shui.

Do sharp-cornered columns or pillars inside the common entrance area cause "poison arrows" or sha qi?

Yes, all sharp-edged columns give off bad energy unless surfaced with mirrors or partly covered with trailing greenery from potted plants. Otherwise, placing evergreen plants near the pointed edge helps to some degree.

My apartment building—rather than my individual apartment—lacks a back door. Does this cause an energy block?

Yes. An apartment building with no back door is like a body with no exit. Check if building management will hang a mirror on a wall where a back door might conceivably be, to form an artificial energy exit.

Does it matter if my apartment faces a staircase or elevator?

Yes. Your home will be hammered by excess energy from these features. Hang a mirror on a wall inside your door to reflect the excess energy back outside.

What other types of "poison arrows" should an apartment resident beware of?

An apartment with another apartment door directly opposite will need fixing with the same mirror cure as in the previous question. Another option is to place a hardy green plant outside your door.

A window view of ugly electrical towers, bridges, or the sharp edges of a nearby freeway is also considered bad Feng Shui. Screen the view or add a Celestial Cure. Window planter boxes often help, too.

How does a view of a large smoking chimney rate?

Many Asian cultures regard a view of two smoking chimney stacks as very bad Feng Shui because of the direct link with the two sticks of incense lit in prayers for the dead. A view of one or three chimneys is not so bad. Western cultures lack this unhappy association. Here the Feng Shui depends more on the degree of ugliness and pollution.

I'm considering buying in a building with a ground-floor or first-floor garage. How does this rate in Feng Shui?

An empty ground floor or first floor is considered bad Feng Shui. Basement car parks are better for the prosperity of high-rise residents.

I'm young and single and live in a "granny flat." Will this affect my life?

It will, so don't refer to your flat as a granny flat, but rather as a studio, garden flat, or some more appropriate name. I recall a letter from a young girl bewildered because she was rarely invited on dates after moving to a granny flat. She tried renaming the flat, but no one else adopted the new name. Later she moved and her dates multiplied.

A person whose own qi life energy is strong may not suffer to the same degree. But it's always best if the subtle influences near you are positive.

Will I be happier buying on top of a skyscraper, or halfway up?

Live half way up for a more stable life. Avoid the top and bottom floors as they expose you to sudden changes of fortune.

Do I need to check the Feng Shui of the communal staircase?

Yes, but check it before you move in, in case regulations forbid adding mirrors, lights, or other cures. A badly placed staircase downgrades the whole building.

I'm single and live in a small apartment. How can I improve prospects for romance?

Add a red and white item, preferably a fan, flowers, candles, or something you personally feel connects with romance, in the Marriage/Relationship position of a Ba-Gua.

If you share an apartment, it may be easier to set up a Ba-Gua in your bedroom, rather than in the living room.

Chapter Nine

Workplace & Office Success

at home & away

When seeking a workplace with good Feng Shui, do previous house guidelines apply?

Yes. Take notice of your first impressions, the quality of qi life energy in the area, and try to find a place around the same height as nearby buildings. Follow all the guidelines in chapters 4 and 5.

Of these guidelines, does any one principle stand out?

Yes. Closely check the fortunes of neighbors and previous building residents. If they went bankrupt or came

119

to a sticky end, think twice about working or locating your business in this place—no matter how low the rent or the asking price.

Is it worth paying more to locate a shop on what Feng Shui calls a "mother," or main, street, rather than a "son," or minor, street?

Usually it is, especially if you're selling fairly basic items.

Can good Feng Shui in my workplace help me win a raise or promotion?

You bet! Talent is only part of the reason people succeed. Knowledge of Feng Shui gives you a distinct career advantage.

What is a Dragon's Mouth office or workplace?

Working in an office or workplace located at the end of a long narrow corridor means you are "looking into the Dragon's mouth." Overly strong qi life energy rushes down the corridor making occupants tired and argumentative.

How can I fix a Dragon's Mouth office?

In Hong Kong, or places where Feng Shui principles are known, the door to an office like this would be moved to avoid attracting bad energy. However, if you screen the door, you can deflect the negative energy. Hanging a wind chime in the entrance or placing evergreen plants here is another remedy.

What is a Dragon Desk of power?

Dragon power in the office flows the same way as in your home. The most powerful place for your office desk lies diagonally across from the door, so you face the entrance.

If your office has several doors, the best desk position offers the most commanding view of all entrances, while situated as far from all doors as possible.

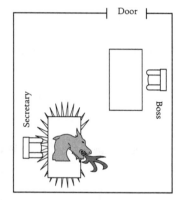

A desk placed in this position becomes a Dragon Desk, giving you added power and zing. Note in the illustration how the secretary occupies the Dragon Desk of power—the boss will gradually lose authority sitting so close to the door. The secretary may well take over!

What is the weakest power position for a desk or workstation?

Sitting with your back to the door or doors, near the door.

Phew! I feel uncomfortable. My boss sits directly opposite me! How can I improve the atmosphere?

This situation can stress the personal qi life energy field of the employee. Harmonize the atmosphere by placing a round bowl of water on your desk, between you and the boss.

To be discreet, you could add flowers to the bowl, but it's the water that counts. A crystal paperweight in the same spot helps your problem, too.

My office door is half glass. Why is this bad Feng Shui?

If you work behind a half-glass door, visitors often see you first, before you see them. Then you lose power.

How do I use a "Rooster Booster" for career success?

A rooster feather placed in your desk drawer gives your career a boost. That's because the rooster is a natural leader, and rooster feathers radiate this same magic power. Roosters are also honored in many, many cultures because their call ushers in the light of morning and understanding, after the darkness of night.

I hate my job but it pays well. How does this affect my personal qi life energy?

Sticking to a job you hate is terrible Feng Shui. It drains your personal qi life energy and keeps you in a state of disharmony. You must work at something you love. Even if the pay is poor at first, your personal qi life energy and health will benefit, and soon you may find ways to increase your pay. Pluck up your courage and quit a hateful job.

Otherwise, take one small action every day toward finding a job in a field you love. One phone call will do.

How do computers affect the energy of a room?

Surprisingly, computers add to the energy of a room. But if you work in a large room chockful of computers, the effect can be overwhelming.

What are good remedies for a room filled with computers?

If you could persuade the boss to add a tiny fountain to the room, everyone would feel re-energized and refreshed. A crystal paperweight on your desk would help, too. And remember an evergreen plant (like a spider plant) near your computer helps remove "electronic smog."

Why do faxes, computers, photocopiers, and other electronic items act up or break down near me?

Feng Shui says there are no coincidences—all events are connected. This occurrence indicates a strong qi life energy upset. Ask yourself, do you really like your job or are you in the wrong place? Is there someone you work with who disturbs you emotionally in some way? Are you hiding this fact from yourself?

Why is a revolving door good Feng Shui?

The rotary movement creates a relaxing and harmonious movement of energy. A rotary overhead fan is good Feng Shui for the same reason.

Sob. At my workplace no one is allowed to change desk or furniture positions. Can I still improve the Feng Shui?

Yes. Hang a mirror on the wall where it reflects the main doorway, or keep a small round mirror in your desk drawer.

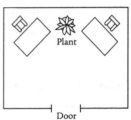

My worst enemy and I share an office. What is a harmonious way to position desks?

The slanted desk position known as a "partial Ba-Gua," shown in the illustration, creates maximum harmony. It's also a good idea to keep a round bowl of water with or without flowers on one desk and a round-leaved plant between desks.

Promotion eludes me. Can I secretly improve my prospects?

Discreetly raise your desk a little above the other desks in your workplace. (You may have to sneak in some small chocks from home.) Likewise, raise your chair. This will be easy with an adjustable chair.

I'm trying to decide between two jobs. Can Feng Shui help?

> Spend a few minutes walking round the foyers, stairs, and corridors of each building. As you walk, sense the atmosphere in each company. It may be busy, friendly, stuffy, cold, formal, or something you can't describe in words. You'll feel more at home or attuned to one place. Choose the place that gives you a greater feeling of personal harmony.

Eeeeek! I'm moving into a jinxed office where one previous resident was fired, another demoted . . .

> This is bad Feng Shui. It's better not to move into such an office, but if it's unavoidable, take extra care with everything you do. Add a Celestial Cure to your office—an evergreen plant, crystal paperweight, desk lamp, or bowl of goldfish.

I sit near elevators. Does this affect my Feng Shui?

> A desk position near rumbling elevators, a downward escalator, or staircase is bad Feng Shui. If you can, add a screen near your desk so you're not looking at these features. Also add evergreen plants or position a wall mirror so it reflects back staircase or elevator energy.

Yawn. Sigh. I need a boost at work. Are there any good luck charms to help?

> Yes. Look up your three cosmically correct Feng Shui lucky charms in chapter 16. You could keep your

Chinese animal zodiac sign and Yang daylight or Yin moonlight lucky charms in your desk drawer, or wear them on your person. For instance, if you are a Boar in the zodiac with a daytime job, place a paperweight of a swan (your daylight or Yang charm) on your desk.

A girl I know, who is a Dog in the Chinese zodiac, works in an all-night carpark. She has stuck rainbow color glass butterflies (her moonlight Yin charm) over the front window of her glass cubicle. Drivers say her sparkling butterfly collection cheers them as they pass. Best of all, these drivers tip her double the amount of other attendants. "The other staff all ask my secret," she laughed. "One even called me a lucky dog!"

I need paintings or prints to brighten my workspace. What themes are good Feng Shui for an office providing financial counseling?

For banks, financial offices, or anyplace dealing with money, choose paintings, wall hangings, or artwork featuring water views. Lakes, seascapes, or rivers are ideal.

What theme should paintings express in education offices?

Landscapes in soft colors are appropriate here.

What theme should paintings express in government offices?

Tradition says good Feng Shui for walls in government offices is brightly colored paintings of water lilies, peonies, or other flowers with large blooms.

I'm a lady cop with her own office in a city police station . . .

Black and white prints or engravings are good Feng Shui for police stations or military offices. The tone of this art can be serious or lighthearted.

What's good Feng Shui for walls in media offices?

Paintings or photographs that feature people, people, people.

I'm starting out in my own law office . . .

Bird studies are good Feng Shui for your walls—but avoid birds of prey, such as vultures or crows.

I worry that my business will be burglarized. Any tips?

For protection, hang two flutes inside the entrance in an inverted V formation. Tie them with red ribbons and keep the mouthpieces down.

How can I use Feng Shui to pep up my profits?

Hang a mirror behind the cash register to expand money energy.

When awaiting a job interview, why should I avoid sitting underneath a light resembling a cluster of five grapes?

Such a light connects with the word "no," and will ruin your chances before you begin.

Why is such a light known as a "Fright Light"?

If you sit under a bad luck light like this during a business meeting, everyone will scorn your ideas.

How does a down-pointing arrow on my shop sign or business card rate?

If you must feature an arrow (and it's better if you don't) point it upward. Chinese people do not like to do business where a sign like this is displayed.

For the Employer

What is an auspicious size for a shop sign or billboard?

A lucky sign is wider than it is high. A square sign is not good Feng Shui. Use three or five colors, not two or four colors.

What desk position sends business downhill and causes a boss to be viewed as a wimp?

A boss who sits near the door will lose status and the respect of the staff. Aim to keep a solid wall behind you, not weakening windows.

What desk positions turn staff into clock watchers?

Staff who sit close to the door will turn into clock watchers, preoccupied with matters away from work.

Does a large column in front of my shop door matter?

If sharp-edged, the column will send bad energy into your shop, reducing prosperity. Place a green plant in front of the sharp edge, or attach a small round mirror above the door frame of your shop to deflect the sha qi, or poison arrows. Mirroring the sides of a sharp-edged column is an Eastern solution, but this may not be possible.

How should I position L-shaped display cabinets?

Ensure the sharp middle section of the L does not point toward the shop entrance. The "poison arrows" repel customers.

I'm setting up a boardroom. Any hints?

Limit the number of doors to two if you want to reduce staff arguments and promote harmony. Multiple doors here resemble and encourage arguing mouths.

The Home Office

Where in our house should I locate my home office?

It depends on the position you want your business to take in your life. If your family complains you are a workaholic, locate your home office toward the back of your house. This will reduce its importance in your mind. When you locate your home office right by your front door, it will assume a larger place in your life.

If you see clients at home, a separate entrance is good, and looks more professional.

How can I improve career success?

Beauty in your workspace inspires and uplifts you. Even if you don't see clients at home, spend a little money creating an attractive, welcoming atmosphere with colors, pleasant lighting, green plants, and prints. Sit at a Dragon Desk position with a solid wall behind you.

If possible, use your Feng Shui lucky charms somewhere in your decor. Occupying a junky, messy, home office will subtly drain your personal qi life energy.

Chapter Ten

The Four Protective House Spirits

harmony during renovations

What are the four protective House Spirits?

Feng Shui says four guardian House Spirits surround your house. When you stand facing out at your front door, the White Tiger prowls on your right, the Green or Azure Dragon roams on your left, the Black Tortoise stands behind, and the Red Bird or Phoenix flies in front.

What surroundings make a perfect or lucky location for the House Spirits?

The ideal model of the four House Spirits gives you an easy way to find a

131

spot with good Feng Shui. A lucky location has either a hill, mountain, or taller building behind, symbolized by the Black Tortoise Spirit with its tough, protective shell. The Green Dragon should sit lower than the Black Tortoise, on the left side.

This means a fortunate site should have a slightly lower hill or building on the left side. The White Tiger should sit a little lower again than the Dragon, on the right side, meaning the building or hill on the right side should be lower than the left side. In front of the house should be a large flat area giving space for the Red Bird or Phoenix to fly.

How do the House Spirits become unbalanced?

In a regularly shaped house, such as a square house that sits centrally in a garden, the four animals are balanced. This causes Yin (passive or female) and Yang (active or male) energy to harmonize.

With an irregularly shaped house, such as an L or T shape, the House Spirits fall out of balance. One House Spirit becomes stronger than the others, who cannot keep it in check. This causes upsets and quarrels for house residents.

We extended our house on one side. How does this unleash the fury of the White Tiger?

Fancy thinking a bad-tempered builder was your only problem!

L-shaped house extensions cause all sorts of trouble. For example, an extension on the right-hand side unsettles the White Tiger and makes him too powerful for the coordinating Green Dragon on the left-hand side to control. The spirit of the White Tiger then prowls your house and garden, causing trouble.

What are the remedies, then?

Add a fountain, garden light, statue, or evergreen tree on the side of your house opposite the extension. This adds more energy and power to the House Spirit ruling that side, and rebalances the situation.

How does an extension on the left-hand side create trouble?

This extension puffs up the Green Dragon, who likewise roams your house and garden causing trouble. Rebalance the energy by placing a fountain, garden light, statue, or evergreen tree opposite the extension to restore power to the White Tiger. Now you see why the ancient Chinese preferred symmetrical houses.

What happens if our front yard is bigger than our backyard?

Sob! This is very bad Feng Shui. Residents in these houses may find friends desert them in times of trouble and they miss out on lucky opportunities. As a remedy, place a magnolia tree, jasmine, loquat, cumquat, or (potted) bamboo somewhere in the front garden to increase favorable qi life energy. Things will soon change for the better.

Our house sits almost on the street. (I bet the House Spirits hate this!) What is the cure?

This is bad Feng Shui—you can see now that the Red Bird House Spirit has no space to fly. Your house should sit at least as far from the road as half the distance of your home's front-to-back length. If not, the road energy will overwhelm you, and life will be a struggle.

Place lamps either side of the front door or add one garden light, preferably a round or curved shape, between the road and front door. This compensates the Red Bird. A wind vane on your roof—featuring a creature of good omen such as a rooster, dove, Red Bird, or Phoenix—is another Celestial Cure for this situation.

What makes the Black Tortoise House Spirit happy?

A back garden larger and higher than your front garden pleases the Black Tortoise. In Feng Shui terms, the Black Tortoise should always sit higher than the Red Bird or Phoenix, the House Spirit who takes care of the house front.

Does if matter if my garden is wider than it is long?

This setup means residents may suffer breathing problems and become psychologically unstable. Balance with a pear, cherry, or camellia tree in your front garden, or a peach tree in the back.

Our block of land is wedge-shaped or wider at the back. How does this influence the House Spirits and us?

Residents will enjoy wealth and unexpected opportunities if the garden widens out near the back of the house, because energy focuses on the area supporting the house.

Our back garden is lower than our front garden? What now?

This means the Black Tortoise House Spirit, which should occupy the highest point at the back of your house, is out of balance and offers you no protection. Life in this house will be unstable unless you add harmonious energy to the back area, with a garden light left on nights. Consider adding a grove of three tall trees at the back of your house. You could fill in the back area to raise it, but this may be costly.

**The stress of renovations often results in divorce.
Any tips to encourage harmony?**

When you live for months in a home where walls are
being ripped down and drastic changes occur, you are
exposed to destructive qi energy. This can depress the
personal qi energy field of all the home's residents.

To rebalance, take weekly time together away
from the center of upset. Linger with a picnic in a
long-established park, or enjoy a formal meal in an
old, traditional restaurant rich with mellow energy.
Avoid trendy new places with the smell of paint in
the air.

Chapter Eleven

Landscape Enchantment

trees, flowers, paths & driveways

How do large trees near my home, workplace, or apartment affect my energy and Feng Shui?

Just like people, trees can be in the wrong place at the wrong time. In the right place, trees increase qi life energy and harmonize the atmosphere. In the wrong place, such as opposite your front door, a tree sends excessive Yin energy rushing into your home causing all kinds of upsets unless remedied as outlined in chapter 4.

Clear away vines entangled in trees because they indicate troubles leading to legal problems or court cases. Tree branches that strain away from a house often indicate weak qi life energy or bad Feng Shui in the house. Y-shaped trees in your front garden indicate conflict between males of the household. V-shaped trees indicate less severe conflict.

Why is a grove of three, six, or nine trees behind a home good Feng Shui? What type of tree is best?

Such trees symbolize the protective mountain, hill, or guardian Black Tortoise House Spirit found behind the ideal Feng Shui house site.

As these trees grow, they guard the welfare of house residents and protect against sha qi, or bad energy. Traditionally, evergreen pine or yew trees make excellent Feng Shui trees. But in this position, any tree beats none, except for willow trees, which should be kept well away from houses.

Is a large tree in front of our lounge window good energy?

Does the tree radiate beauty? Then it's good. But take action if the tree radiates gloom or blocks a lovely view. Also, if sunlight—Yang, or active, energy—shines brightly through the leaves, it neutralizes the excess Yin energy of the tree. If no sunlight filters through, hang a small mirror above your window frame to deflect problem energy.

Which three trees emit harmonious energy as a group and are traditionally called the "Three Friends of Winter?"

Pine, plum, and bamboo. They all bring good Feng Shui to your garden and win a special mention in the famous Chinese garden at Darling Harbor in Sydney, Australia.

Pines symbolize long life and emit strong and revitalizing qi life energy, helpful to invalids or for anyone feeling low. Relax under one for an afternoon if you need a boost. Bamboo casts dancing shadows that bring beauty and elegance to your garden—confine it to a large pot, as it spreads quickly. The pretty blossoms of the flowering plum cheer you as they herald the end of winter.

Do tree stumps on a property signal good or bad Feng Shui?

A tree stump is not good Feng Shui. Grow ivy or vines near the stump base and trail greenery across the top. This prevents bone or teeth trouble for nearby residents. And be wary if you see decayed tree stumps just under the soil.

Is it okay to leave a dead tree in our garden?

No. Get rid of it, or you invite bad Feng Shui.

Is one large jutting rock in a garden bad luck?

Yes. Submerge the jutting rock more deeply into the soil, or build up the soil around it. Then add two medium-sized rocks nearby.

Spread yogurt on the rocks to encourage the growth of tiny plants, such as mosses.

When do rock gardens and winding paths create good Feng Shui?

If a swimming pool takes up most of your garden area, excess Yin energy can overwhelm your house. Adding rock gardens rebalances with Yang energy. Winding paths increase overall harmony.

Why is an all-white flower garden bad Feng Shui?

White flowers symbolize death and mourning. Add multicolored bright flowers to rebalance your garden. Otherwise, go for pastels.

Which flowers combine Yin and Yang qualities?

The begonia and viburnum possess this rare feature.

What are the special good luck flowers?

Peonies, chrysanthemums, plum blossom, magnolia, and narcissus.

What type of garden best attracts peace and harmony?

A garden with soft curving lines that echo nature. Add soothing water in the form of a pond, preferably containing goldfish, or a fountain, waterfall, or birdbath. If you lack funds even a large above-ground urn or container filled with water improves the Feng Shui.

Make sure your garden contains seats and tables that invite you to relax. Then close your eyes and listen. If need be, add harmonious sounds: splashing water, humming insects, birdsong, or wind chimes.

We inherited a garden with military-style straight lines. Can we make it more harmonious?

Add curving lines with garden arches, flower beds, or a kidney-shaped or round pond.

Where's the best position for our front garden gate?

The left, or Dragon, side of your house when you stand at your front door looking out. If your garden gate runs in a line with your front door, a winding path between slows the passage of qi life energy.

Are there dangers when positioning a storage shed?

Yes, storage areas accumulate stagnant qi energy, so don't position the door of the storage area opposite your front door.

This would allow stale energy to enter your house, resulting in quarrels and missed opportunities. If your storage shed already occupies such a spot, lock its door and either add another shed door or turn a shed window into a door.

Is a house covered in creeper good Feng Shui?

A small amount of creeper or vine on a building is good Feng Shui as it symbolizes attunement with nature. But a house *smothered* by creeper is bad Feng Shui, as nature then dominates.

There's a very long narrow cement path at the side of our house. How can we improve its Feng Shui?

Qi life energy rushes too quickly along such a path. Add curved garden arches covered in vines or flowers at intervals along the path.

I'm a keen gardener and hostess. Can you suggest a lucky Feng Shui feature for my garden?

How about a lucky octagonal herb garden, or an eight-sided pavilion or gazebo? Or a shrub in your back garden clipped into the shape of the Tortoise House Spirit, which guards this area?

What is the remedy for bare, high walls in a garden?

Looking on to bare walls invites money troubles, so train quick-growing vines or flowers up the wall. Jasmine often suits. No soil? Try potted plants, or ask an artistic friend to paint a cheery wall mural of flowers, plants, or a happy scene from nature.

What is the most fortunate shape for a garden path?

By now you should know—circular, semicircular, or curving.

Is a zig-zag path preferable to a long, straight path?

Yes, it discourages the passage of sha qi or problem energy.

The approach to Chinese temples often features a zig-zag path.

What shape driveway attracts wealth to a home?

A circular driveway is best, followed by a semicircular driveway. Notice how often homes of royalty or the rich and famous feature these shapes. Change your driveway if at all possible! It doesn't have to be paved.

What shape driveway strangles money flow?

A thin, straight line. The longer your drive, the worse the result.

Our farmhouse drive is peculiar! It narrows down near the road. Is this good Feng Shui?

It's bad Feng Shui because the smaller entrance near the road reduces qi flow. Change the shape or install two lights on posts near the road.

Chapter Twelve

Water Wisdom

swimming pools, ponds & prosperity

Do water views near home or workplace attract money?

Yes. A waterfront view invites money to come to you, and it's best if the water moves gently rather than lies stagnant. However, when a lake, canal, river, or even the ocean lie behind your house, it's usually weakening to residents. You may see moneymaking opportunities, but be unable to benefit from them.

How can I double the benefit of water views?

Hang a mirror where it reflects the water view into your house.

Does my swimming pool or garden pond encourage wealth?

Yes, as long as the water is clean. Straight-sided pools must be correctly positioned. Pool corners should not point toward the home (see illustration opposite).

Why is dirty pond or pool water bad Feng Shui?

Dirty water nearby invites money to come to you, but often it will be tainted money, obtained unlawfully, and resulting in trouble.

What is the luckiest shape for a pool, pond, or fountain base?

Circular, kidney, curved, or octagonal.

How must a kidney-shaped pool curve to hold in luck?

The pool should curve toward the house as if embracing it, as illustrated. (Note the Y-shaped tree in the illustration. Happily, it's at the back of the house.) A pool curving the other way lets luck escape.

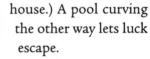

When does a straight-sided pool emit poison arrows?

When the edge of a sharp-angled pool points directly toward a house, it emits sha qi or destructive energy.

Place evergreen shrubs between the sharp edge and house, as shown in the illustration.

Use potted plants if the area is paved. A fountain between pool and house is another remedy.

Is it better not to have a pool, than to have a rectangular one?

No, because ponds and pools near your home still invite prosperity. It's easy enough to fix a rectangular pool with a cure.

Our swimming pool takes up almost all our back garden area and lies very close to the house. Does this affect our Feng Shui?

Yes. House residents will tend to be overwhelmed by water qi, and can become sickly. Rebalance by installing a rock garden on any tiny bit of land area and make sure any garden paths wind and curve. Window coverings looking onto the pool should be yellow as this is the color of the Earth element, and helps block water qi.

Does the position of my swimming pool or pond matter?

Yes. When you view your house block as one whole unit or shape, a pool or pond activates the corresponding area of the I Ching Ba-Gua in which it is positioned.

So a swimming pool in the left-hand back corner of your block will further activate the Ba-Gua Prosperity area, while a swimming pool in the right-hand back corner will improve the Ba-Gua Marriage or Relationship area of your life.

I recently visited the house of a famous Australian actor in Melbourne. He secretly follows Feng Shui. Decked in red bathers, he showed me his swimming pool, designed to strengthen his Fame area using the correct colors of red, yellow, and green.

The pool is a good Feng Shui kidney shape, curving toward his mansion. It's tiled in yellow with shimmering green water and his initials on the bottom in red. "I struggled mightily to get green water rather than blue," he said. "I avoided explaining my reasons to the down-to-earth pool builder."

What is a Prosperity Pond?

Many Feng Shui followers place a small pond in the back left-hand corner of their property to strengthen the Prosperity area of their block.

Where should I place my pool to improve family life?

If you check the I Ching Ba-Gua diagram in chapter 3, you'll realize this swimming pool should be placed midway along the left-hand side of your block of land, in the Family area.

A small island sits in the middle of our ornamental pool. How does this affect the Feng Shui of house residents?

Badly. Add an ornamental bridge crossing to the island, otherwise one person in the house will become isolated from the others. For the same reason, do not place one large single rock in the middle of your pond.

Any further tips on improving the energy of ornamental ponds?

Imitate the gentle charm of nature where possible. Soften the edge of the pond with a fringe of over-hanging plants or rocks, rather than display a rim of bare concrete. Add darting goldfish and water lilies (their round shapes are auspicious) for further good Feng Shui.

Keep relaxing garden seats nearby so you're tempted to sit by your pond and dream.

Chapter Thirteen

The Color of
Good Feng Shui

with an ancient warning on clutter

**What colors best promote harmony
and peace?**

Pale pastels bring out the best
Feng Shui in a room. Pale peach
and pale apricot are particularly good.
Even modern psychology agrees that
pastels create harmony, and recom-
mends soothing peach tones for
hospitals, nursing homes, and jail
interiors.

As single colors, red, green, and
gold all radiate the best Feng Shui.
The Chinese call red "the color of
happiness."

151

Which colors are Yin and which are Yang?

All colors are either Yin or Yang. Yin colors are mainly green, blue, purple-blue, and gray. The primary Yang colors are red, yellow, purple-red, and orange.

Why should I beware of all-white houses, rooms, and clothing?

White drains energy and connects with mourning, death, and bad luck. In the West, all-white homes, kitchens, and bathrooms have been fashionable for a while—but beware!

In Australia, casino managers planned to supply millionaire Asian gamblers with free white limousines to ferry them round town. But these luck-conscious high rollers refused to travel in white limos.

I need a quick uplift for an all-white house exterior . . .

Add a strong color, such as dark green or burgundy, on exterior areas such as trims, guttering, window shutters, awnings, or blinds.

I know pale peach has extra good Feng Shui. Is it a good idea to repaint my entire interior this one color?

An entire interior of pale peach is extreme. It's always better to balance Yin and Yang. For greater harmony, add one contrasting color or material, perhaps in a wood trim.

What clothing colors boost personal qi life energy?

Again, avoid all-white, or add a splash of color in the form of a scarf or accessories. In Hong Kong, dentists and dental nurses, who wear white uniforms, are recommended by Feng Shui experts to wear revitalizing red ribbons around their wrists in the evenings.

If you wear a white uniform, counteract the drain by wearing red underwear, or red somewhere on your person.

Men who feel depressed should wear brighter, happier colors when possible. Their somber work colors of black, gray, brown, and white drain their personal qi life energy field. At least switch white to cream, and add bright or pastel splashes in shirts, ties, and socks. Many famous actors always wear red socks for luck.

Yikes! I'm going for my driving license test and need extra confidence and zip. What color should I wear?

If you're feeling afraid, wear a bright red, cherry, or scarlet item of clothing, like a blouse or jacket, to charge up your personal qi life energy field or aura. One small red handkerchief is insufficient, but red underwear will help. A new item of red clothing also works better than an old item.

Did you know that even Julius Caesar wore a red cape, to help give him courage, when he went into battle? Often we know intuitively what will help.

I need guidelines for interior furnishing . . .

Don't plan everything using cold logic—allow intuition full play. Some Feng Shui followers use a pendulum to choose between two pastels. Chapter 14 shows you the way.

How can I improve the Feng Shui of a gloomy room?

Add a skylight, paint the interior pale cream, peach, apricot, or lemon, and add pale flowers. An extra light bestows harmonious energy, too.

Blush! I overheard someone whisper my house lacks soul and resembles a bland hotel interior . . .

Your home will have more character and better Feng Shui if it reflects the true personality of its residents. Rather than choose prints, paintings, or artworks by unknown artists, buy one from a friend or someone local. Handmade items are also good Feng Shui; so are cherished collections. Whether you collect shells, china plates, or tiny dolls, make a lively display near the entrance. Guests find this a fascinating talking point.

Don't aim for a perfect house. Display that lopsided vase your child made in school or the chess set your son carved—even if the pieces lean to one side. These items reflect love and harmonize your home.

Can some modern art create bad Feng Shui?

Yes. Some modern art looks ugly or disturbing, and many fashionable themes portray conflict or violence. Over time, these plant the same seed of conflict in your home. Even the famous ancient Greek philosopher Plato felt art was healthier if it portrayed harmony.

Everyone suffers enough stress—choose soothing or beautiful art for your home. Leave disturbing pieces to museums and galleries, rather than displaying them in your everyday living space.

Where should I place a portrait of my great grandfather?

Move the old boy from the dining room, kitchen, or places where food is eaten or prepared. Photos or portraits of ancestors emit Yin energy, so are best in living rooms, where energy is Yang.

Why is it good Feng Shui to display musical instruments?

Musical instruments represent harmony. They create serene and happy energy in your home or workplace. Flutes top the list.

How does our collection of antique pistols and swords rate?

Shudder! They are bad Feng Shui, creating the energy of conflict in your home. Newspapers often carry reports of normally peaceful people who, in the heat of an argument, grab an antique weapon displayed nearby and kill or seriously injure someone. Afterward everyone marvels how this gentle person did such a terrible thing.

Recently I read about a normally gentle, elderly teacher who stabbed her husband to death using an antique weapon from a wall display. Knowledge of Feng Shui could have prevented this tragedy.

Where should I place my dragon statue?

When you stand at your front door looking out, position your dragon on the left-hand side—the side the Dragon House Spirit guards. Many people with open fireplaces like to place these fire-breathing creatures by the hearth. Others prefer their dragons near the entrance of their home.

Where in our home should I place my tiger print?

When you stand at your front door looking out, the Tiger House Spirit guards the right-hand side of your house. So place it wherever feels good on the right hand side. However, if you are a Rabbit, or one of the smaller animals in the Chinese zodiac, some experts say you should not hang a tiger print. Its energy is too strong for your sign. I say if you like tigers, it's a sign you can coexist, but do give the matter some thought.

Where should I place my new lamp, for good Feng Shui?

If you need light for clarity in one spot, place the lamp there. If you aim more for good Feng Shui, check your Ba-Gua positions and decide which one you wish to activate. Or you may wish to fix a problem, like a door at the Prosperity area, with a pretty light.

A dear friend who visits yearly gave me a scowling statue that I feel has bad Feng Shui. She'd be hurt if I didn't display it.

Between your friend's visits, wrap this statue in gold silk as insulation. Keep it out of sight, away from your home—in a suitcase in a garage is ideal.

Are there any Feng Shui principles on positioning clocks?

Yes. Do not place clocks so they can be seen by anyone who opens the front door.

Why is clutter bad Feng Shui?

A famous Chinese sage warns, "Qi energy moves like a dancer and cannot abide a cluttered stage." In other words, clutter blocks the flow of qi life energy, tiring residents and keeping them stuck.

Why does clutter near a front door invite big trouble?

Your front door is the main entrance for qi life energy to flow into your home. If it is blocked with clutter, such as old furniture or newspapers awaiting disposal, house residents will also feel blocked and tired. Hoarding clutter symbolizes fear of the future.

Yawn. I'm worn out. How can I get fresh new energy?

Silly as it sounds, take fifteen minutes to clean out and order just one drawer of a desk or cupboard. Discard or give away anything unneeded. Right after you'll feel a burst of fresh energy. (Just imagine the boost if you clean out an entire room!)

Never clean out large areas at a time. You'll end up giving up. Spend no more than fifteen minutes to half an hour a day clearing a room of junk.

Chapter Fourteen

Magic Feng Shui Rituals

easy steps to better luck

How can I marry or attract a proposal within eighteen months?

First, ask a married friend to give you a cup—this transfers marriage qi energy to you. Buying a cup won't do. Then buy a gold-colored wedding ring, it doesn't matter how cheap. In the daytime, keep this ring on your bedside table in the cup, along with nine grains of rice and a red ribbon eight inches long (or eighteen centimeters long—not the same in length, but chosen for the influence of the lucky "love" number eight).

Every night before you sleep, place the ring on your finger, just as you would a wedding ring. Go to sleep feeling the ring on your finger, imagining or feeling you're already married. Try to really capture this feeling every night. If you miss an occasional night, don't worry. Within eighteen months you should be married, or have received a proposal.

I can't guarantee you will marry your current boyfriend, if you have one. Many people report someone completely new coming into their lives, or a much-loved old flame may return out of the blue.

I don't know any married people well enough to ask for a cup. Will another item make the previous ritual work?

No, this is a rare case when you must follow one rule. Feng Shui is subtle and clever—the fact you mix only with single people might be part of your problem.

There must be married neighbors or people nearby you could get to know. Mull over your associates. Relatives and family will do, too!

We've tried for ages to have a baby. Can the Feng Shui Baby Boost method help?

Many overjoyed readers have sent success stories and baby photos—you may be next!

The Chinese Art of Placement says it's important to prepare a special room or place for baby and start to furnish it as though you are already expecting. If possible, keep this room away from your front door, toward the back of your house. (Hopefully your own bedroom is located here, too.)

Next, place eight grains of rice overnight in the main doorway of your living room, or the room that feels like the "heart" of your home. Then put an item of yellow or white baby clothing in the Ba-Gua Children position of your living room—the center of the wall to the right of the door you regard as your main living room door. This encourages favorable cosmic forces.

Use only yellow and white, as these colors harmonize with the correct section of the I Ching Ba-Gua, an Eastern guidance symbol dating back thousands of years.

Feng Shui lore also says that when you want to become pregnant, never dust under the bed. Dusting disturbs the *ling*, or spirits of hovering unborn children. And once you are pregnant, don't move house until after the baby is born.

What's the ancient remedy to attract more attention from the opposite sex?

To win more dates, place a small round mirror under your mattress. A powder-compact size is fine.

Important facts and names slip my mind. I need . . . um, what was it? Oh yes, the Memory Magic technique!

The Yin Door, or Black Door, technique helps anyone with this problem. When you're struggling to remember anything, breathe in and out slowly and deeply, taking longer on the out-breath, to relax yourself.

Then close your eyes and imagine a black door in front of you. Concentrate on the color black for about thirty seconds to a minute. (Visualize your black hand-bag or shoes if you find this difficult.) Now go about your day and stop trying to remember. The answer will pop effortlessly into your mind later, through the Yin Door, when you're busy on other tasks.

At first, the technique may take hours to work. After a few times, it often works in minutes.

Oops! I smashed a mirror. Can I avoid seven years' bad luck?

Buy a tiny mirror roughly the same shape, not size, as the broken one. A handbag mirror will do. Paint the back green or cover it with green paper. Now take it to the nearest crossroads you can find, where you see bare earth rather than cement. Bury the small mirror in a little soil nearby, and pour a glass of water over it. Then replace the soil. The wind and water will now take your bad luck away from you, to vanish down the crossroads.

Groan. My sore back makes me feel older than Confucius.

Place nine pieces of pastel chalk with a little uncooked rice in a pastel-colored china or glass bowl. Position the bowl under the bed, near your back. Remove the bowl each morning and replace it each night. Expect a marked improvement or cure any time after the first night.

How do I take a romantic Pearl Bath?

All bathrooms come under the influence of the mighty Water Dragon, and all Dragons dine on nothing but pearls. Happily, Dragons are not picky eaters—they don't insist on Cartier pearls! Even a fake pearl from a discount store or broken necklace makes a tasty snack.

To encourage the Water Dragon to bestow good fortune on you—or grant a romantic wish—simply drop a pearl into your bath water when preparing for a special event or a glamorous evening out.

You can only feed the Water Dragon this way once a year, and it's best to let the pearl vanish with your bath water. Otherwise bury it later, preferably near light-colored flowers.

How do I chase away the blues in a couple of minutes with the Feng Shui Red Bird and Rainbow recipe?

You'll enjoy this Red Bird Daydream from a very modern Feng Shui consultant. It sounds simple, but the effect is powerful. Close your eyes. Slowly breathe out, then breathe in and out four times, taking much longer on the out-breath. This relaxes you.

Now imagine a friendly Red Bird flying up to you with a beautiful rainbow plucked from the sky. Wind this rainbow round your neck and body like a scarf, and feel cheered. Stay with this feeling for around half a minute. Now open your eyes. Go about your day imagining you still wear your rainbow scarf.

Spend only two to three minutes on this and the following exercise. You won't improve the effect by spending longer.

I have a scary task to perform. Can Feng Shui help?

You bet. This daydream exercise might sound childish, but the image of your White Tiger House Spirit radiates very powerful energy and quickly helps you feel more courageous. Try it when you need to confront a school principal, return faulty goods, or ask for a pay raise.

As before, close your eyes and breathe in and out four times, taking longer on the out-breath. Now imagine a friendly White Tiger, the guardian spirit of the right side of your house, prowling over. He looks ferocious to everyone but you. See yourself taking your White Tiger on a leash when you set off for your scary task. Sense the new mood of courage this gives you and stay with this feeling for about half a minute. Now open your eyes and return to everyday life.

What is the Feng Shui cure for warts?

Warts are mysterious in the way they come and go! First, dab the warts with half a cup of warm water in which a pinch of ginger has been dissolved. Place a silver coin and as many small pebbles as you have warts inside a piece of red cloth tied up with red ribbon.

Leave the bag some place open to wind and water, such as on a fence post or windowsill. After it has rained nine times on the bag, the warts will go. Then bury the bag near an exit door, such as a back garden gate. This ensures the warts depart for good.

A previous tenant committed suicide in our house. How do I cleanse the bad energy?

A surprising number of people live in a house where a murder or dreadful accident occurred. If you feel you must move, go ahead. But often this is impossible and then the following classic Feng Shui ceremony will help.

Place the skins of nine lemons, grapefruit, or oranges in a china bowl and cover them with boiling water. When the water cools, sprinkle or spray it lightly round the boundaries of the place where the unpleasant event occurred.

To further improve the Feng Shui, change the color of the room to the opposite end of the spectrum. For instance, if the room is blue change it to a warm-toned pastel like apricot, or vice versa.

I hate chopping down a tree, but its position opposite our front door is bad Feng Shui. It might fall on our house, too. What is the traditional harmonizing ceremony to perform before cutting trees down?

Feng Shui lore says if you recklessly chop down a tree, you can expect trouble with your teeth. To prevent misfortune, mix ninety-nine drops of newly opened red wine with something silver, such as a coin. Sprinkle the lot around the tree base, before chopping. And if possible, plant something new in your garden, however small, as compensation.

If a tree stump remains, grow ivy near the base and trail it across the stump. Otherwise, nearby house residents may experience trouble with their bones.

We argued bitterly with our house builders, leaving "bad vibes." How do we perform the protective Feng Shui Earth-turning recipe before moving to our new land?

Carry out this ancient ritual as soon as possible—hopefully before digging extensively in your new garden.

Mix ninety-nine drops of newly opened red wine with nine dessert spoons of uncooked rice and as many silver items as corners on your property. Then add another two silver items. Silver coins are fine.

Sprinkle the red wine and rice very thinly round the boundaries of your block of land. Then bury a silver coin in each corner and one either side of the driveway or main entrance.

How do I restore healing properties to a large crystal I've dropped and chipped?

To restore healing properties, leave your crystal on a windowsill overnight during the next full moon. If you can't wait until then, dip the crystal into natural seawater, which you should collect in a glass, china, pottery, or ceramic dish. Otherwise, leave the crystal sprinkled with sea salt overnight. (Health food shops usually carry sea salt.)

How do I cleanse crystals used for Feng Shui purposes?

Never soak crystals in hot water, as this damages them. From time-to-time, cleanse them by passing them through a cloud of incense. You can make your own from burnt, dried orange peel with a dash of sage.

Job interviews make me nervous. Any tips?

The Chinese Art of Placement explains that you're uncomfortable at job interviews because you're in an unfamiliar psychological and physical place.

To solve the first problem, apply for jobs you don't want as practice, so you'll feel more relaxed in interviews. Write down your seven major job strengths and aim to communicate them in the shortest possible time.

To help with the second problem, visit the place where the interview will be held—hopefully at least several days before the event. When you return, Feng Shui says you'll feel more comfortable.

The Jade Necklace recipe that follows will help, too.

My personal qi life energy and confidence feel low and I'm about to go to an important event. How can I recharge?

Feng Shui Grandmaster Professor Vincent Wu calls this his "Jade Necklace recipe." He says every compliment you receive is like a gift of a precious jade bead. The trouble is most of us lose these precious balls of happy energy soon after they're given to us. Their restorative power vanishes.

Buy a pretty jade-green notebook and write down every compliment you remember anyone giving you and every new one you receive. Now you have a string or necklace of precious jade beads, with the power to uplift and harmonize you.

Read over your list of compliments before you go somewhere scary to restore your confidence and personal qi energy. This also boosts your energy when surrounded by draining, negative people (modern-day vampires!).

What should I beware of when grooming myself in mirrors?

Don't subconsciously criticize your looks. This creates a black cloud of destructive qi energy all round you. Your mirror then reflects and magnifies this gloom out into the world, depressing others in the house as well.

Make it a habit when looking in a mirror to focus on three features you like about your looks—even it it's just your shiny hair or the flattering color you're wearing.

Now you're surrounded with golden qi life energy, which your mirror will reflect and magnify. You'll feel happier, and so will those around you.

How do I use a pendulum to get answers to questions?

Use a pendulum when you need answers from the intuitive part of your mind, rather than the cold, logical part. Not everyone will feel attracted to this technique, but try it if you can't decide between two colors or a decorating scheme. Feng Shui says the unknown part of your mind often knows better than the rational part.

As a weight, use any item heavy enough to swing freely. Choose a ring, single bead, crystal, pointed piece of jewelry, or small item of hardware.

Attach your chosen weight to a length of thread or chain—roughly seven inches, or around seventeen centimeters, long is fine. Trial and error will show what length feels comfy. Sit with your elbow resting on a table and let the pendulum hang from your thumb and index fingers.

Hold your pendulum and notice how it can swing four ways: horizontally, vertically, clockwise, and counterclockwise. Think "yes" for about two minutes and see which way your pendulum begins to swing. Then think "no" and check which way it swings. These are your personal directions. They will be different for everyone.

You can also establish directions by asking your pendulum a question to which you know a yes-or-no answer, such as, "Are my eyes blue?"

If you don't succeed at first, try again when you're more relaxed. Some people give the pendulum a little twitch to start if off but it usually begins moving soon after you ask a question. Remember to concentrate on the question, not the expected answer.

Chapter Fifteen

Strange & Spooky

unusual feng shui questions

I suspect I have a house ghost. What now?

If you feel unhappy about a house ghost as a house guest (many people live happily with them) change the main door position in the room the ghost inhabits. If a ghost roams your whole house, change the position of the front door. House ghosts then become confused and disoriented. No longer feeling "at home," they depart. Leaving a light on all the time in a haunted room is another cure—a mini-crystal chandelier works really well.

If you just want protection, hang one or two flutes where the presence feels strongest.

My car was in an accident. Can I fix the bad vibes?

This is a surprisingly common problem and, yes, there is a Feng Shui cure, adapted from a traditional bad-energy remedy. Cover the skins of nine lemons, grapefruit, or limes with boiling water. Let the water cool, then flick or spray it all around the car interior. Be sure to include the steering wheel and car tires.

If you feel extremely uneasy, change your car's color to the opposite end of the color spectrum.

Can I practice Feng Shui without realizing? I find I naturally follow many principles.

Yes, and congratulations on your finely tuned intuition—an ability closely connected to Feng Shui. Many people instinctively hang a mirror above a fireplace mantelpiece and seat guests correctly in Honored Guest or Dragon Seats of Power, which face the door.

Any special Feng Shui tips for newlyweds?

Certainly. Your first home together is a magical place and lives in your heart long after your confetti has scattered to the four winds. Enjoy it *now*. Spend freely on small furnishing luxuries you both adore. Don't live in the future, saving madly for a grand mansion five years down the track.

I'm confused. I read an American book claiming metal wind chimes should never be used . . .

In every batch of a hundred experts, one always seems to disagree with the other ninety-nine! For instance, an occasional medical expert claims smoking won't harm your health and an occasional skin expert claims scoffing three boxes of chocolates won't affect your skin. It's the same in Feng Shui.

Rest assured, metal wind chimes are fine. Half the wind chimes in the world are made of this substance. As long as they emit a harmonious sound, they bring excellent Feng Shui.

What are lucky numbers for my car number plate, or elsewhere?

Use a mix of eight and nine in any combination that feels good. In Hong Kong people pay huge sums for these numbers on car plates. 168 and 68 are deemed extremely fortunate, as are 66 and 88.

What's the round Feng Shui compass with peculiar markings called? Do I need one?

A *luopan*. You won't need one with international Dragon Door Feng Shui.

I work in a casino and get stressed because of all the numbers I have to remember. Can Feng Shui help?

Yes, strange as it sounds, you need to breathe like one of the House Spirits, the Black Tortoise, slowly and deeply. Feng Shui masters say to be more relaxed and live longer, observe the animals. A dog breathes quickly and lives an average of ten to fourteen years but a tortoise breathes extremely slowly (only once every five minutes in certain cases), and some live to 150 years.

Wear jewelry featuring a tortoise to remind yourself.

I need a name with good Feng Shui to boost the success energy of my baby . . .

It's always better Feng Shui to choose an unusual name, even one you make up, as it will radiate fresher stronger qi life energy, guiding your baby toward success. Just like old cheeses, names can get worn out and pass their expiration date!

This doesn't mean you can't succeed with a popular name—but it will be harder.

Tiger Woods, the famous golfer, grabs masses of media limelight because of his wonderful first name Tiger which just bursts with good Feng Shui. Without this name, success would probably have come slower. Celebrity Oprah Winfrey is also helped by her first name.

I live in a motor home. How can I improve my energy and luck?

Often motor homes, or caravans, have only one door which can cause an energy blockage, resulting in upsets and quarrels. Hang a long slim mirror on a back wall, so that it forms an artificial exit for blocked energy. You'll notice the improved atmosphere right away.

Caravan stoves are usually well positioned so you can cook facing the door in the Peaceful Cook position. If you can't, hang a wind chime near the caravan entrance.

We live on a yacht. Any Feng Shui tips for us?

Yachts are surrounded by overwhelming Yin, or female, energy from all that water. To counterbalance with Yang energy, paint the yacht interior any shade of lemon, yellow, or pale apricot. Timber paneling looks great, too.

The worst thing about yachts in Feng Shui terms? Most cabins sit "down below." I find when you venture down, you often feel as though you're stepping into a cellar, cut off from the lively moods of wind and water.

Raise the floor levels in cabins down below so you can see out windows or portholes when standing. Do the same for the saloon table and seating area. Keep ceilings pale colored and, if possible, increase the size and number of portholes. Try to keep bench and table shapes curved rather than rectangular, or with sharp edges.

Watch lighting—one of the Nine Celestial Cures. Too often it's too weak on yachts I've checked, which creates disharmony and gloom. Install strong lights above the head of each bunk, and make sure there's a large mirror down below to act as an artificial back door and prevent energy blocks and quarrels.

On long water voyages, wear yellow clothing, also the color of the Earth element, to block water qi and brighten your spirits.

Why do many Chinese dislike the number four?

Because the word "four" sounds like "die" in Chinese. For this reason many hotels in Hong Kong do not have a fourth or fourteenth floor. Strictly speaking, it's not part of Feng Shui but Chinese superstition.

Some Asians will not consider buying a "number four" house, the way some Westerners would not consider living in a "number 13." Those trying to sell a "four" house could add a mini-fountain near the street number, but there are no guaranteed remedies for this mindset. You need to find a buyer not concerned with numbers. They do exist. Many happy, wealthy people live contentedly in number four houses.

Keep in mind that four also links to rebirth and connects with romance, arts, and literature.

I'm house-hunting in a roaring hurry. Quick!

One main tip . . .

Choose a place you love on first impression. Don't rely only on logic. Yes, this could mean you'll live in a houseboat or loft!

I've been stuck in a rut for years. How do I improve my life?

Your problem amounts to being in the one place for too long—you become stale and your qi energy field weakens. To change your life for the better, the Chinese Art of Placement suggests you now change the position of twenty-seven items in your life, including yourself. Shop at a new supermarket. Take a different route to work or wherever you regularly visit. Go somewhere completely new each week, like an evening class in a subject that interests you.

When you feel stuck, you also need to get rid of clutter.

As the years pass, does the Feng Shui of my home change?

Usually it does, because all things change, including our surroundings. Different buildings or tall towers may pop up around you, new influences may appear like different neighbors, or a vacant block, park, or school opposite your home. Keep watch with Feng Shui cures, so your environment stays in balance.

I've remarried and will live in the same house where my husband previously lived most unhappily. How can I change the house aura without huge costs?

Change the color of the front and back door to the other end of the spectrum. For example, if they're now pale cream, change them to bright red, or get wooden doors.

As soon as you can afford it, repaint inside the house using the same principles. Hang a wind chime near your front door and carry out the age-old citrus cleansing ritual in chapter 14.

What are the three most important Feng Shui checks in a house?

Ensure your bed and kitchen stove are well positioned, and no "poison arrows" attack your front door.

How can we improve the Feng Shui of our racehorse stable?

Many stables feature a long central passageway dividing the horse stalls. This can allow qi life energy to travel too quickly, so hang a wind chime halfway along to improve the energy flow. Horses get bored easily and will enjoy the sound. Keep a radio at the Ba-Gua Prosperity area in the stable and switch it on for a few hours each day to stir up the qi life energy. Make sure there's plenty of air and light, and allow the horses plenty time out of the stables, too.

World-famous racehorse trainer Bart Cummings used various Feng Shui techniques in 1996 with Melbourne Cup winner Saintly. Saintly won a grand prize that day of over 1.3 million dollars!

What's an unusual gift with good Feng Shui for the housewarming of a friend who has everything?

A wind vane featuring a rooster, horse, dragon, or creature of positive omen is both good Feng Shui and fashionable. Recently, wind vanes have become hot collector items. Even Steven Spielberg has one!

The circular motion of the vane on top of the house makes it a Celestial Cure, inviting harmonious energy to house residents. It would be wonderful if you could match your friend's Chinese animal zodiac birth-year sign. They're given in chapter 16.

My Feng Shui question is not listed. How can I solve it?

Sit in silence daily for ten minutes with your eyes closed and listen. Eventually you will tune into your inner wisdom, particularly if you sit at the I Ching Ba-Gua Wisdom area of a room, or somewhere you find beautiful, preferably in nature. After a while the answer will come to you out of the blue.

Can we use Feng Shui to hurry the sale of our house?

Yes. Take a photo or ad for your house, stick a green or red SOLD sign across it and place it at the I Ching Helpful People point of the Ba-Gua. Keep the picture in a black and white frame, or with black and white ribbons nearby. Look at the photo for a couple of minutes first thing in the morning and last thing at night. And stop talking of items being hard to sell—this muddies your surrounding qi life energy field.

If I only remember one important thing from this entire book what should it be?

Whenever you get a faint feeling of unease, it's a warning of bad Feng Shui, meant to help you. Take note. It doesn't matter whether the feeling involves a house, person, event, or place.

A famous Australian university academic (one of few to survive a hideous crocodile attack) said recently that when she first entered the area where the croc later attacked she ignored "a very faint sense of unease."

Soon after, she was grabbed in the jaws of the croc, savaged, and spun in a death-roll underwater. Miraculously, she survived.

She concluded that civilized living makes us ignore these faint, helpful feelings, and vowed from then on to listen to them.

Another person told me when she first passed a little office in Melbourne belonging to a certain financial organization, she vaguely mused how she disliked its name. The office gave her a tiny bad feeling.

Six or seven years passed, the organization acquired glamorous new offices and the woman forgot all about her first faint feeling of unease. She invested heavily with this company along with many others. The organization crashed and the woman's money was tied up for ages, while investors fought for justice. "If I'd known about Feng Shui, I would have saved myself a lot of heartache and purse-ache," she sighed.

Remember these examples whenever you get a faint feeling of good or bad Feng Shui. This ancient Eastern art is very subtle. But it will assist you greatly in your journey through life, in ways you cannot begin to imagine!

Chapter Sixteen

Yin Moonlight
& Yang Daylight

your lucky charms

Does luck really exist?

You bet! Otherwise, how do you explain situations where some people win the lottery not once but twice, plus minor prizes as well. Statistics say, "Impossible!" Yet with some people it happens. Luck showers them with blessings, so they lead a charmed life.

How many different types of luck exist?

The Chinese, who have collected good luck secrets since the second century B.C., classify luck in three ways. Your Celestial luck or destiny is written in the heavens—you can't do much about this. Then there's your Yang or daylight luck and your Yin or moonlight luck, which can be improved with cosmically correct lucky charms.

To enhance your earth luck, you can also adjust your working or living space according to the rules of Feng Shui.

How do lucky charms encourage good fortune to smile on you?

Your Yang (daylight) and Yin (moonlight) lucky charms connect on a cosmic basis with your Chinese animal zodiac sign—which corresponds to your birth year. Wearing your lucky charms or placing them in your environment helps harmonize your energy field to attract positive forces.

Harmony is one of the seven major power forces in the universe. It attracts all good things to come to you: peace, prosperity, happiness, health, joy, luck, and love.

Can my lucky charms bring me confidence on special occasions?

Definitely. Swags of letters to my column prove this is one of the main reasons people enjoy owning their lucky charms. When you feel nervous or need reassurance for a special event, from a job interview to a court case or glamorous night out, wear your lucky charms, or tuck them into your bag.

The longer you own your lucky charms the stronger and more individual their accumulated lucky qi force becomes. That's why you should never lend your charms to another. Your lucky charms work a third way, too—they help neutralize bad luck coming your way.

Which rich and famous people in history believed in luck?

Let's name just a few. The great Napoleon always enquired first of any likely associate, "Has he luck?" If the answer was "No," Napoleon avoided or would not hire the person. And American John Paul Getty—a millionaire by age twenty-two—called all his early successes "pure luck." Likewise, the fabulously wealthy Rothchilds believed strongly in luck and advised, "Never have anything to do with an unlucky place."

What are Yin moonlight and Yang daylight lucky charms?

Yin and Yang are Eastern names for the two opposite but equal forces in the universe. Each of the twelve traditional animal signs in the Chinese zodiac has a matching Yin moonlight and Yang daylight lucky charm.

What is my Chinese zodiac animal sign?

The following short list appears worldwide in magazines and newspapers. Look for your birth year and find the corresponding sign.

Dog: 1922, 1934, 1946, 1958, 1970, 1982, 1994, 2006, 2018

Boar: 1923, 1935, 1947, 1959, 1971, 1983, 1995, 2007, 2019

Rat: 1924, 1936, 1948, 1960, 1972, 1984, 1996, 2008, 2020

Ox: 1925, 1937, 1949, 1961, 1973, 1985, 1997, 2009

Tiger: 1926, 1938, 1950, 1962, 1974, 1986, 1998, 2010

Rabbit: 1927, 1939, 1951, 1963, 1975, 1987, 1999, 2011

Dragon: 1916, 1928, 1940, 1952, 1964, 1976, 1988, 2000, 2012

Snake: 1917, 1929, 1941,1953, 1965,1977, 1989, 2001, 2013

Horse: 1918, 1930, 1942, 1954, 1966, 1978, 1990, 2002, 2014

Sheep: 1919, 1931, 1943, 1955, 1967, 1979, 1991, 2003, 2015

Monkey: 1920, 1932, 1944, 1956, 1968, 1980, 1992, 2004, 2016

Rooster: 1921, 1933, 1945, 1957, 1969, 1981, 1993, 2005, 2017

What are my matching Feng Shui Yin and Yang lucky charms?

Animal	Daylight Yang	Moonlight Yin
Rat	Piano	Harp
Ox	Teapot	Bell

Animal	Daylight Yang	Moonlight Yin
Tiger	Scissors	Shoe
Rabbit	Cat	Boat
Dragon	Key	Pearl Ring
Snake	Turtle	Bird
Horse	Duck	Hat
Sheep	Lantern	Sea Creature
Monkey	Masks	Moon
Rooster	Money Sack	Wine Bottle
Dog	Mandolin	Butterfly
Boar	Swan	Water Fairy

Why are those born in the first six or seven weeks of our Western year known as Double Happiness or Double Blessings people, when it comes to their lucky charms?

These people are in an unusual and fortunate situation. If they wish, they can choose between two Chinese lucky charm signs. This is because of up to seven weeks' difference between the Chinese and Western years. (The Chinese year is not fixed like ours. It can start anytime January to mid-February.)

Magazines and newspapers round the world commonly print the Chinese zodiac animal signs in a short version, which roughly corresponds to our Western years. Thus 1962 would generally be known as a Tiger Year. Someone born that year would have Yang and Yin lucky charms of a pair of scissors and a shoe.

However, imagine you are born in the first six or seven weeks of 1962. Look up the detailed Chinese calendar given in the Appendix, see page 193. (Millions of Westerners never bother.) You may find you are classified here under the previous year Chinese animal zodiac sign, rather than that given in the short list commonly printed.

So if you were born in 1962 anytime up to February 4, you are, in the detailed Chinese year calendar, still actually in the Year of the Ox, with different lucky charms.

However, many Chinese astrologers and Feng Shui Masters agree, along with judges in legal systems, that common usage by millions of people changes outcomes. So, even those born in the first six or seven weeks, come heavily under the influence of the Tiger through mass usage and association.

To sum up, people born in the first seven weeks can choose the set of Yin or Yang lucky charms they prefer.

Ask yourself which animal zodiac sign feels more you? Which animal you like best is often a clue. Or you may prefer to check the broad characteristics of each sign. Otherwise, as the Chinese say, ask yourself which animal hides in your heart.

Many people I know in this category use all six lucky charms for the two signs!

Is there a story behind every group of three Feng Shui lucky charms? I'd love to hear a few . . .

Yes, there are—some short and some long. The Tiger charms, for instance, feature a shoe and a tiny pair of scissors. The shoe connects with the foot, which for a prowling speedy tiger is a source of luck and strength. Scissors refer to the power of the almighty tiger to "cut off" life.

The ox, teapot, and bell lucky charms connect to a Chinese myth. This tells of a lucky ox who owned a magic teapot and never had to plough the field like other hardworking oxen. All good things poured from this teapot—food, drink, silver, gold, love, and luck.

One full moon while the lucky ox slept, the other earthbound oxen tried to steal this celestial teapot. But each night the lucky ox removed his neck bell and hung it near the teapot. When the bell tinkled the lucky ox awoke and escaped with his teapot into the heavens. Any full moon, if you look in the right part of the northern sky, you may see the ox, lucky teapot, and bell outlined in the stars. (At time of writing not all the stories behind each set of charms have been translated from the original Chinese.)

Is it wise to wear my Yang charm only in the daylight and Yin charm only in the moonlight?

Use your intuition. Each set of charms feels different to each owner. Some people do like to match their charms to either moonlight or daylight wear. Other people wear all three charms all the time.

I'm a Tiger and my moonlight lucky charm is a shoe. Does it matter what sort of shoe I choose?

No. For Tiger shoe charms I've seen a tiny high-heeled shoe, a miniature gold sandal, a cowboy boot, a fun sneaker, and an exquisite ice skate shoe in gold and white enamel. All invite good fortune.

Does it matter which substance lucky charms are made from?

No. But, understandably, many people prefer gold, silver, crystal, or precious stones.

I'm in a nerve-wracking court case. Are my lucky charms okay tucked inside my bag?

Yes. Your charms don't need to be visible to bring you luck.

Can lucky charms be used in room decor or other ways?

Certainly. In your office, you could use a large version of a charm as a paperweight. This adds good qi life energy to your surroundings and neutralizes the effect of cranky coworkers.

A smaller charm like a butterfly might be used as a brooch, key ring, or ornament. Or you might prefer an entire collection of framed butterfly paintings, as a wall display.

How can I feature my baby's lucky charms in our nursery?

Use them in a cute mobile to dangle above baby's head, on a wall frieze, as cot motifs, wall picture, or blanket border or even embroidered onto baby's clothing.

One nursery I saw for a baby Boar featured an imaginative wall mural of a lake with swans and water fairies. The fairy also starred as the base of baby's night lamp. There's no end to the way you can apply Yin moonlight and Yang daylight lucky charms.

How can I discreetly incorporate my husband's lucky charms in his workplace?

If your husband works in an office in the daytime, how about a gift of a paperweight in his daylight Yang charm? For instance, a male Snake could be given a brass turtle paperweight.

A male Horse I know is thrilled with the jade duck paperweight his wife gave him for his home office.

Is a collection of lucky charm items good Feng Shui?

And how! You'll find there's something almost magical about collecting things. When friends hear about your passion, they send you additions from everywhere, even from their overseas travels.

Lucky charms seem to swarm in your door under their own steam.

Is it true that England's Queen Elizabeth collects lucky charms?

Yes, and they are mostly gifts from her children. Many have an animal theme, and her collection includes miniature dogs (she loves corgis), horses, saddles, and riding shoes. Collecting lucky charms is definitely a royal habit!

Where can I obtain my official Feng Shui lucky charms that connect with my Chinese zodiac animal sign?

If you would like to invest in your three Feng Shui lucky charms in precious sterling silver, including your Yin moonlight and Yang daylight sign, check out my Web address:

www.luckycharms.magshop.com.au.

Each set of official Feng Shui lucky charms has been placed on my own personal Ba-Gua for extra good fortune.

I'm flat broke. How can I improve my prosperity?

List the moneyed places in your area. In the city it will be certain uppercrust suburbs or foyers of ritzy hotels. Once a week or so stroll around these places for at least an hour and soak up the prosperous qi life energy.

The Art of Placement says do this regularly and you'll absorb prosperous new ideas and thoughts. You'll also notice little lucky events start happening to you. Soon these lucky events will multiply and grow.

If you live in a small town or the country, buy or borrow from your library one lavish glossy magazine showing the best in cars, furniture, jewelry, or houses. The American magazine *Architectural Digest* is ideal. Spend an hour a week enjoying the pictures. This will start lifting you out of your "poor place" consciousness. You could also place a few wall pictures of luxury items in your bedroom, at the Prosperity area.

Any other easy ways to improve luck that doesn't cost a cent?

Certainly. Deliberately mix with happy, fortunate people whose lucky qi energy will rub off on you.

Assess your associates. Avoid those who always complain and criticize. And if you're a single female: beware of doom-and-gloom men who want to take you out for "whining and dining." Luck prefers companions like joy and harmony.

Appendix: Discover Your Birth-Year Element

Oops—what are the Five Elements again?

The Five Elements are five basic moods, patterns, or qualities of qi life energy. Though they are called Wood, Fire, Earth, Metal, and Water, these are symbolic names, not the actual substances. Each element controls or nourishes one other of the Five Elements.

What does my birth-year element reveal about me?

In brief, those born under Fire tend to be decisive, confident, and natural leaders. Their downside is selfishness or violence. Earth people are solid and reliable, with overcaution as their downside. Those born under Metal are usually goal oriented and independent, with a flip side of rigidity. Water people communicate well. Sensitive and flexible, they sometimes lack backbone. Wood people are hardworkers with executive ability. Their other side? Arrogance or gloom.

Happily, knowledge of Feng Shui helps bring harmony and balance to all the elements.

Year	Sign	Element	Year Begins
1900	**Rat**	Metal	**31 Jan 1900**
1901	**Ox**	Metal	**19 Feb 1901**
1902	**Tiger**	Water	**8 Feb 1902**
1903	**Rabbit**	Water	**29 Jan 1903**
1904	**Dragon**	Wood	**16 Feb 1904**
1905	**Snake**	Wood	**4 Feb 1905**
1906	**Horse**	Fire	**25 Jan 1906**
1907	**Sheep**	Fire	**13 Feb 1907**
1908	**Monkey**	Earth	**3 Feb 1908**
1909	**Rooster**	Earth	**22 Jan 1909**
1910	**Dog**	Metal	**10 Feb 1910**
1911	**Boar**	Metal	**30 Jan 1911**
1912	**Rat**	Water	**18 Feb 1912**
1913	**Ox**	Water	**6 Feb 1913**
1914	**Tiger**	Wood	**26 Jan 1914**
1915	**Rabbit**	Wood	**14 Feb 1915**
1916	**Dragon**	Fire	**3 Feb 1916**
1917	**Snake**	Fire	**23 Jan 1917**
1918	**Horse**	Earth	**11 Feb 1918**
1919	**Sheep**	Earth	**1 Feb 1919**
1920	**Monkey**	Metal	**20 Feb 1920**
1921	**Rooster**	Metal	**8 Feb 1921**
1922	**Dog**	Water	**28 Jan 1922**
1923	**Boar**	Water	**16 Feb 1923**
1924	**Rat**	Wood	**5 Feb 1924**
1925	**Ox**	Wood	**24 Jan 1925**
1926	**Tiger**	Fire	**13 Feb 1926**
1927	**Rabbit**	Fire	**2 Feb 1927**
1928	**Dragon**	Earth	**23 Jan 1928**
1929	**Snake**	Earth	**10 Feb 1929**
1930	**Horse**	Metal	**30 Jan 1930**

Year	Sign	Element	Year Begins
1931	Sheep	Metal	17 Feb 1931
1932	Monkey	Water	6 Feb 1932
1933	Rooster	Water	26 Jan 1933
1934	Dog	Wood	14 Feb 1934
1935	Boar	Wood	4 Feb 1935
1936	Rat	Fire	24 Jan 1936
1937	Ox	Fire	11 Feb 1937
1938	Tiger	Earth	31 Jan 1938
1939	Rabbit	Earth	19 Feb 1939
1940	Dragon	Metal	8 Feb 1940
1941	Snake	Metal	27 Jan 1941
1942	Horse	Water	15 Feb 1942
1943	Sheep	Water	5 Feb 1943
1944	Monkey	Wood	25 Jan 1944
1945	Rooster	Wood	13 Feb 1945
1946	Dog	Fire	2 Feb 1946
1947	Boar	Fire	22 Jan 1947
1948	Rat	Earth	10 Feb 1948
1949	Ox	Earth	29 Jan 1949
1950	Tiger	Metal	17 Feb 1950
1951	Rabbit	Metal	6 Feb 1951
1952	Dragon	Water	27 Jan 1952
1953	Snake	Water	14 Feb 1953
1954	Horse	Wood	3 Feb 1954
1955	Sheep	Wood	24 Jan 1955
1956	Monkey	Fire	12 Feb 1956
1957	Rooster	Fire	31 Jan 1957
1958	Dog	Earth	18 Feb 1958
1959	Boar	Earth	8 Feb 1959
1960	Rat	Metal	28 Jan 1960
1961	Ox	Metal	15 Feb 1961

Year	Sign	Element	Year Begins
1962	Tiger	Water	5 Feb 1962
1963	Rabbit	Water	25 Jan1963
1964	Dragon	Wood	13 Feb1964
1965	Snake	Wood	2 Feb 1965
1966	Horse	Fire	21 Jan 1966
1967	Sheep	Fire	9 Feb 1967
1968	Monkey	Earth	30 Jan 1968
1969	Rooster	Earth	17 Feb 1969
1970	Dog	Metal	6 Feb 1970
1971	Boar	Metal	27 Jan 1971
1972	Rat	Water	15 Feb 1972
1973	Ox	Water	3 Feb 1973
1974	Tiger	Wood	23 Jan 1974
1975	Rabbit	Wood	11 Feb 1975
1976	Dragon	Fire	31 Jan 1976
1977	Snake	Fire	18 Feb 1977
1978	Horse	Earth	7 Feb 1978
1979	Sheep	Earth	28 Jan 1979
1980	Monkey	Metal	16 Feb 1980
1981	Rooster	Metal	5 Feb 1981
1982	Dog	Water	25 Jan 1982
1983	Boar	Water	13 Feb 1983
1984	Rat	Wood	2 Feb 1984
1985	Ox	Wood	20 Feb 1985
1986	Tiger	Fire	9 Feb 1986
1987	Rabbit	Fire	29 Jan 1987
1988	Dragon	Earth	17 Feb 1988
1989	Snake	Earth	6 Feb 1989
1990	Horse	Metal	27 Jan 1990
1991	Sheep	Metal	15 Feb 1991
1992	Monkey	Water	4 Feb 1992

Year	Sign	Element	Year Begins
1993	**Rooster**	Water	**23 Jan 1993**
1994	**Dog**	Wood	**10 Feb 1994**
1995	**Boar**	Wood	**31 Jan 1995**
1996	**Rat**	Fire	**19 Feb 1996**
1997	**Ox**	Fire	**7 Feb 1997**
1998	**Tiger**	Earth	**28 Jan 1998**
1999	**Rabbit**	Earth	**16 Feb 1999**
2000	**Dragon**	Metal	**5 Feb 2000**
2001	**Snake**	Metal	**24 Jan 2001**
2002	**Horse**	Water	**12 Feb 2002**
2003	**Sheep**	Water	**1 Feb 2003**
2004	**Monkey**	Wood	**22 Jan 2004**
2005	**Rooster**	Wood	**9 Feb 2005**
2006	**Dog**	Fire	**29 Jan 2006**
2007	**Boar**	Fire	**18 Feb 2007**
2008	**Rat**	Earth	**7 Feb 2008**
2009	**Ox**	Earth	**26 Jan 2009**
2010	**Tiger**	Metal	**10 Feb 2010**
2011	**Rabbit**	Metal	**3 Feb 2011**
2012	**Dragon**	Water	**23 Jan 2012**
2013	**Snake**	Water	**10 Feb 2013**
2014	**Horse**	Wood	**31 Jan 2014**
2015	**Sheep**	Wood	**19 Feb 2015**
2016	**Monkey**	Fire	**9 Feb 2016**
2017	**Rooster**	Fire	**28 Jan 2017**
2018	**Dog**	Earth	**16 Feb 2018**
2019	**Boar**	Earth	**5 Feb 2019**
2020	**Rat**	Metal	**25 Jan 2020**

Index

Free Magazine

Read unique articles by Llewellyn authors, recommendations by experts, and information on new releases. To receive a **free** copy of Llewellyn's consumer magazine, *New Worlds of Mind & Spirit,* simply call 1-877-NEW-WRLD or visit our website at www.llewellyn.com and click on *New Worlds.*

LLEWELLYN ORDERING INFORMATION

Order Online:
Visit our website at www.llewellyn.com, select your books, and order them on our secure server.

Order by Phone:
- Call toll-free within the U.S. at 1-877-NEW-WRLD (1-877-639-9753). Call toll-free within Canada at 1-866-NEW-WRLD (1-866-639-9753)
- We accept VISA, MasterCard, and American Express

Order by Mail:
Send the full price of your order (MN residents add 7% sales tax) in U.S. funds, plus postage & handling to:
Llewellyn Worldwide
P.O. Box 64383, Dept. 0-7387-0291-9
St. Paul, MN 55164-0383, U.S.A.

Postage & Handling:

Standard (U.S., Mexico, & Canada). If your order is:
$49.99 and under, add $3.00
$50.00 and over, FREE STANDARD SHIPPING

AK, HI, PR: $15.00 for one book plus $1.00 for each additional book.

International Orders (airmail only):
$16.00 for one book plus $3.00 for each additional book

Orders are processed within 2 business days.
Please allow for normal shipping time. Postage and handling rates subject to change.

Feng Shui for Beginners
Successful Living by Design

RICHARD WEBSTER

Not advancing fast enough in your career? Maybe your desk is located in a "negative position." Wish you had a more peaceful family life? Hang a mirror in your dining room and watch what happens. Is money flowing out of your life rather than into it? You may want to look to the construction of your staircase!

For thousands of years, the ancient art of feng shui has helped people harness universal forces and lead lives rich in good health, wealth, and happiness. The basic techniques in *Feng Shui for Beginners* are very simple, and you can put them into place immediately in your home and work environments. Gain peace of mind, a quiet confidence, and turn adversity to your advantage with feng shui remedies.

1-56718-803-6
240 pp., 5¼ x 8, photos, diagrams $12.95

101 Feng Shui Tips for the Home

RICHARD WEBSTER

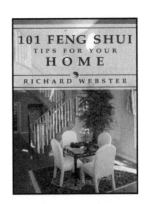

For thousand of years, people in the Far East have used feng shui to improve their home and family lives and live in harmony with the earth. Certainly, people who practice feng-shui achieve a deep contentment that is denied most others. They usually do well romantically and financially. Architects around the world are beginning to incorporate the concepts of feng shui into their designs. Even people like Donald Trump freely admit to using feng shui.

Watch your success and spirits soar when you discover:

- The best color to paint your kitchen
- Where to sit your dinner guests to encourage a friendly atmosphere
- How to arrange your living room furniture
- Colors to use and avoid for each member of the family

1-56718-809-5
192 pp., 5 ¼ x 8, charts $9.95

Spanish edition:
Feng shui para la casa
1-56718-810-9 $7.95

To order, call 1-877-NEW-WRLD
Prices subject to change without notice

Gemstone Feng Shui

**Creating Harmony
in Home & Office**

SANDRA KYNES

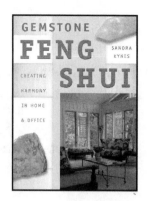

Feng shui meets crystal therapy! Each area of a room (and your entire house) represents an aspect in your life that can be affected by the gemstone you place in that area.

Draw on the powers of gems to unlock your potentials and counteract negative energy in your environment. You will learn the basic concepts and tools of feng shui and the various attributes and uses of specific gemstones.

0-7387-0219-6
240 pp., 6 x 9, 93 tables, 26 illus. $14.95

Spanish edition:
Feng Shui con gemas y cristales
0-7387-0267-6 $14.95